Glossary of Floriculture and Landscape Architecture

The Authors

Krishna S. Tomar is working as an Assistant Professor (Floriculture and Landscaping) in the Department of Floriculture and Landscape Architecture, College of Horticulture, Banda University of Agriculture and Technology, Banda, Uttar Pradesh. He has served at two constituent colleges of Central Agricultural University, Imphal, Manipur including College of Horticulture and Forestry, Pasighat, Arunachal Pradesh for 13 years in different capacities. He has vast practical experience in floriculture and landscaping and he is associated in teaching, research and extension for the last 15 years including 7 years in teaching. He has published 20 research papers in National and International Journals of repute, 1 book, 3 manuals, 5 book chapters, 45 Popular Articles, 20 Abstracts and has presented research papers in international, national workshops, seminars and symposia. He also delivered 3 T.V. Talks.

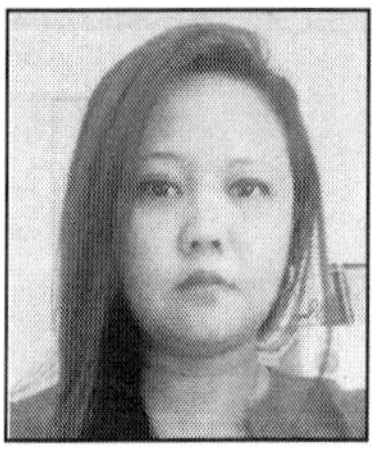

Kalkame Ch. Momin is working as Assistant Professor in the Department of Floriculture (Ornamental and Medicinal Plants), College of Horticulture and Forestry, Pasighat, Arunachal Pradesh under Central Agricultural University, Imphal, Manipur. She worked as a Guest Lecturer in the Department of Horticulture, North Eastern Hill University. Dr. Momin has over 20 articles, book chapters, manuals *etc.*, and has presented papers in international, national workshops, seminars and symposia.

T.S. Mehra is working as an Associate Professor (M and AP) in the College of Horticulture and Forestry, Central Agricultural University, Pasighat, Arunachal Pradesh. During this period he served as Head of the Department of Floriculture (Ornamental and Medicinal Plants) for more than seven years and is involved in teaching, research and extension activities in the field of medicinal and ornamental plants. Owing to his vast experience Dr. Mehra has published more than 40 articles, 4 manuals and 6 bulletins, book chapters, folders *etc.*

Ajay Kr. Singh is working as an Associate Professor (Floriculture and Landscaping) in the Department of Floriculture and Landscape Architecture, College of Horticulture, Banda University of Agriculture and Technology, Banda, Uttar Pradesh. He has served as SMS/Assistant Professor (Horticulture) at G.B. Pant University of Agriculture and Technology, Pantnagar, Uttarakhand for 11 years. He has published 20 research papers in National and International Journals of repute, 1 book, 4 manuals, 2 book chapters, 40 Popular Articles, 30 Abstracts. He also delivered 5 Radio Talks and 2 T.V. Talks.

Glossary of Floriculture and Landscape Architecture

Krishna S. Tomar

Assistant Professor
Department of Floriculture and Landscape Architecture
College of Horticulture, Banda University of Agriculture and Technology
Banda, Uttar Pradesh

Kalkame Ch. Momin

Assistant Professor
College of Horticulture & Forestry, Central Agricultural University
Pasighat, Arunachal Pradesh

T.S. Mehra

Associate Professor
College of Horticulture & Forestry, Central Agricultural University
Pasighat, Arunachal Pradesh

Ajay Kr. Singh

Associate Professor & Head
Department of Floriculture & Landscape Architecture
College of Horticulture, Banda University of Agriculture and Technology
Banda, Uttar Pradesh

BIOTECH

2021

BIOTECH BOOKS®

ISBN 978-81-7622-446-8

Published by: **BIOTECH BOOKS**®
4762-63/23, Ansari Road, Darya Ganj,
New Delhi - 110 002
Phone: 09899295259
E-mail: biotechbooks@yahoo.co.in

Typeset at: **Classic Computer Services**
Delhi - 110 035

Printed at: **Replika Printing Press**

PRINTED IN INDIA

This small endeavour dedicated to

Our Beloved Parents

who provided us an ample opportunity for acquiring the advanced knowledge in our respective disciplines.

Dr. S.L. Goswami
Vice Chancellor

BANDA UNIVERSITY OF AGRICULTURE & TECHNOLOGY, BANDA-210001, U.P. INDIA

No. VC/2018/345 Date 28/08/2018

Foreword

Flowers are intricately entwined in the social fabric of our nation and no function is complete without flowers. Floriculture is considered as one of the most diversified and potential component of horticultural industry. Modern floriculture is practiced globally while Indian floriculture remained traditional to a great extent with homestead farming. Today, floriculture industry in India is characterized by growing traditional flowers, cut flowers, bedding plants, plug plants, fillers, trees, grasses, foliage and flowering potted plants besides producing dry flowers, annual flower seed and planting material, value added products like essential oils and nutraceutical pigments. In ancient era, the flowers were used mainly for religious offering but now the floriculture sector has attained the commercial status and has emerged as a big venture. There is a dynamic shift from sustenance production to commercial production in this era and thereby significant increase in trade of flowers at domestic level because of rapid urbanization, increase in income level, etc. Flower business is considered as a most lucrative business as commercial floriculture has higher potential per unit area than most of the field crops.

In the last three decades the education and research in floriculture and landscape architecture has attained new heights. Floriculture and Landscape Architecture is an integral part of course curriculum being taught at undergraduate levels in disciplines of Agriculture, Horticulture and allied sciences in various universities across the nation. Moreover a number of SAUs and CAU are also offering PG and PhD programme in Floriculture and Landscape Architecture as a separate discipline. This stream is considered as a major component for competition point of view *e.g.* in ICAR-JRF. SRF, ICAR-NET. ICAR-ARS and Assistant Professorship in SAUs and CAUs. It has been felt for long time that the latest technical terms pertaining to Floriculture and Landscape Architecture subject were not available in compiled form. This Glossary covered all the updated and latest terms on Floriculture and Landscape Architecture and it would be very helpful for the students, research scholars and aspirants appearing in various competitive examinations.

I congratulate the authors for bringing out the book 'Glossary of Floriculture and Landscape Architecture' which will certainly be useful to students, researchers, scholars, teachers, amateur garden lovers and stakeholders involved in floriculture and landscaping.

S.L. Goswami

Preface

Floriculture is emerging as most diversified and potential component in horticulture industry owing to its rapid growth rate, increasing purchasing power and awareness among the masses. It is one of the fastest growing sectors in domestic and international trade and holds high business potentials and prospects. Nowadays, it is the key component in the trade of diversified range of products, *viz.* cut flowers, loose flowers, dried flowers and their products, bulbs and tubers, pot plants, nutraceutical and pharmaceutical compounds, essential oils, natural colourants, plug plant production, protected cultivation, seed production, tissue culture, nursery, *etc.*

This glossary is a selective compilation of more common technical terms used in floriculture and landscape architecture and is recorded here as an aid to both the floriculturists and the garden enthusiasts who do not have ready access to many well prepared glossaries. The glossary includes all descriptive terms used in floriculture and landscape gardening found in one-easy to use handbook. The ornamental gardening world is filled with all sorts of unusual terms and jargon and it is confusing for anyone new to the subject. While most of the people recognise these terms, there may still be some uncertainty about certain terms and what it implies. This glossary aims to outline the common terms related to flowers, gardening and landscaping to improve the understanding of terms in a better way. There are some technical terms that are related to landscape architecture, which even the experts or students with strong vocabulary may not be aware or familiar with words and this book gives such a list of words for the benefit of all. The authors took all out efforts to bring together terms from various books, monographs, technical manual, web resources, *etc.*

The leading author express his sincere gratitude to Dr. S. L. Goswami, Hon'ble Vice Chancellor, Banda University of Agriculture & Technology, Banda, UP who assigned him various responsibilities of landscaping works of the university and honing his skills in floriculture and landscaping and he is also grateful to Prof. N. K. Bajpai, Director of Extension and Prof. S.V. Dwivedi, Dean, College of Horticulture, Banda University of Agriculture & Technology, Banda for their unflinching moral supports and creating amicable environment at BUAT, Banda. The senior author is thankful to Dr A. K. Pandey, Dean, College of Horticulture and Forestry, RLBCAU, Jhansi, UP (Ex Dean, CHF, CAU, Pasighat) for showing his faith upon him while working at CHF, CAU, Pasighat.We express sincere thanks to Ms. Gaby Gao, MTS, CHF, CAU, Pasighat, Arunachal Pradesh for typing the manuscript meticulously. We appreciate the efforts of Mr. Sunil Mittal, M/s Biotech Books, New Delhi for publishing the book. Last but not the least; our beloved students have always been instrumental for us in questing new words in the domain of floriculture and landscaping.

We are hopeful that this 'Glossary of Floriculture and Landscape Architecture' will immensely be useful to the students and experts; to the former as providing a concise definition and to the latter as a reminder of a word or term employed in a special sense.

Krishna S. Tomar

Kalkame Ch. Momin

T.S. Mehra

Ajay Kr. Singh

A

2H-budding: A double rectangular cutting, resembling the letter H, made in the bark of the stock. The flaps are lifted in the centre for insertion of the bud.

2n: The chromosome number of the somatic cell of a species.

Abiotic pollination: Transfer of pollen by abiotic means, such as wind (Anemophily), water (Hydrophily), on the water surface (Epihydrophily), under the water surface (Hypohydrophily), and gravity (Geitonogamy).

Abortion (flower): The failure of a bulb to develop perfect flower after formation of the floral organs.

Abscise: Fall off, as of a leaf or petal falling off the flower

Abscission: Shedding of plant parts as a result of the formation of an abscission layer of loosely adhering cells at its base which breaks apart readily; regulated by abscissic acid.

Absolute: It is highly concentrated, entirely alcohol soluble and usually liquid perfume material.

Acaricide: A chemical that kills mites and ticks; miticide.

Accent or focalization: The feature which first attracts the eye is known as accent or focal point or focalization. That feature may draw attention through its form (shape), habit, colour, size, texture, sound, motion, *etc.* The hidden focal point is called as vista. This may be created through a specimen plant, flowers, statues or fountains.

Acclimatization: Gradual process of establishment of a plant in a new locality in which environmental conditions differ markedly from those of its native habitat.

Achene: A small, hard, dry, indehiscent fruit, strictly of one free carpel.

Acridity: Sense of irritation in tasting different aroids due to the presence of needle like crystals of calcium oxalate in the different plant parts of the aroids (Taro, Elephant foot yam, *etc.*).

Acropetal: Development of organs in succession towards the apex, the oldest at base, youngest at tip, *e.g.*, leaves on a shoot.

Acropetalous: Leaves or flowers growing sequentially from the base of the plant or stem towards apex.

Actinomorphic flower: Regular flower *i.e.*, when petals, sepals, stamens, *etc.* are equal and more of less equidistant so that the flower may be cut into two equal halves through any plane.

Active ingredient (a.i): It is a part of a pesticide formulation which is the actual toxicant sometimes referred to as "technical grade" or "basic pesticide"

Acuminate: Narrowing to a sharp point with sides having curvature, such as leaf shape of *Ficus religiosa, Holarrhena, etc.*

Acute: Pointed apex in the form of an acute angle, but not stiff, as the leaf shape of china rose, mango *etc.*

Add Value: The processing of raw products into secondary products the latter being more expensive than the former.

Adenosine diphosphate (ADP): A compound made up of adenine, five carbon sugar ribose and two phosphate groups which are involved in the mobilization of energy in cellular metabolism.

Adenosine tri phosphate (ATP): It is ADP with an additional phosphate group attached by a high energy bond and its decomposition into ADP and phosphate results in the release of energy needed by cellular metabolism.

Adjuvant: Additives, as chemicals added to a preservative to enhance its effectiveness

Adnate: Union of members of different floral whorls, *e.g.*, petals with stamens, or stamens with carpels, as seen in orchid.

Adventitious buds: Buds or shoots arising from any plant part other than terminal, lateral, or latent buds on stems.

Adventitious embryony: A type of apomixes where the embryos arise from a cell or a group of cells either in the nucellus or in the integuments outside the embryo sac in addition to the regular sexual embryo, seen in *Citrus, Opuntia, etc.*

Adventitious roots: Roots arising from any plant part other than the seedling root and its branches.

Aeration: A method of improving soil infiltration and air penetration of compacted soil by for example removing small cores of soil.

Aerial roots: Roots that arise above the ground, from either the stem or the base of the plant.

Aerophyte: A plant that grows on another plant but is not parasite on it, *e.g.*, some types of orchids like *Rhynchostylis retusa.*

Aestivation: It refers to the arrangement of the sepals and petals in a flower bud.

After Ripening: A period after harvesting required by certain fruits to complete embryo maturity.

Agameon: A species that contains only apomictic individuals.

Agamotropic: Used of flowers that do not close again once they have opened.

Agar: A gelatinous and complex polysaccharides obtained from sea weeds (*Gracilaria* sp., *Gelidium* sp., *etc.*) widely used as a substrate in aseptic cultures and making jelly, ice cream, soap, pastries as emulsifier.

Ageing: A process involving increment of time which is generally accompanied by physiological changes.

Agriculture: An activity of man which is primarily aimed at the production of food, fibre, fuel, *etc.* by optimum use of terrestrial resources.

Air storage: Storage in the room at normal air temperature providing proper air flow and ventilation which facilitates the removal of ethylene produced by fresh fruits and vegetables and maintains the CO_2 and O_2 level about 0.03 and 21.0 percent, respectively.

Air-layering: A method of layering which consists of removing a ring of bark from one to two-year-old shoots and covering the cut from surface with a rooting medium, after which the rooted layer is separated from the parent plant; practiced in guava, litchi, lime, *etc.*

Air-lock: Bubble of air in the cut stem which causes obstruction in the flow of water resulting premature wilting of cut flower.

Albinism: Absence of chlorophyll in a green plant.

Albino plant: Plants having no green tissue.

Albuminous seed: Seeds in which endosperm is large and contains most of the food materials.

Allee: A very formal design of planting trees lining both sides of a path or drive.

Allele: One of pair of genes at the same locus on homologous chromosomes.

Allelopathy: Production of allelochemic substances by certain plants that is harmful to other plants, such as juglone from walnut and terpenes from soft chaparral which inhibits germination of seeds or roots of other plants.

Alley cropping: A farming system in which arable crops are grown in alley formed by trees or shrubs mainly to hasten soil fertility restoration and enhance soil productivity.

Alliance: A tribe or group of related genera. Among orchids many of these genera can crossbreed with other genera.

Allophillic blossom: The flower with no morphological adaptations unique to a specific pollinator, hence, accessible for any pollinator.

Alluvial soil: A soil developed from recently deposited alluvium with no horizon development or modification of the recently deposited materials.

Alternate: An arrangement of stems, leaves, or buds which are spaced singly along the length of a branch, rather than in pairs (opposite).

Amateur Gardener: A person who grows and arranges flowers and ornamental plants for personnel satisfaction and not for financial gains is known as an amateur gardener.

Ambient: Normal room temperature.

Amenity planting: The planting of trees to add to one's comfort and convenience or to the attractiveness of the area, shed trees, ornamentals, windbreaks *etc.*

Ament: A soft spike of small petalfree flowers of only one sex which, when it has completed its function, drops as a unit. See Catkin.

American Colonial Period: A simple style of floral design in the colonies (pre United States) that combined fresh and dried materials in arrangements.

Ammonium fixation: The adsorption or absorption of ammonium ions by the mineral or organic fractions of the soil in such a manner that they are relatively insoluble in water and relatively non exchangeable by the usual methods of cation exchange.

Amphidiploids: An allopolyploid containing two copies each of two or more distinct genomes (4X, 6X, *etc.*) and as a consequence behaves as a diploid during meiosis.

Amphihaploid: Plant having a haploid set of chromosomes from each parent of an interspecific hybrid, thus being 2X rather 4X as in case of an amphidiploids.

Amphimixis: The normal sexual reproduction in which the morphologically dissimilar male and female gametes unite together to form the zygote.

Analogous Colour Scheme: It is achieved by using closely or harmonious colours such as violet with blue and light blue with green and yellow with green, or yellow with yellow orange.

Analogues: Analogous (sometimes called harmonious) color schemes are any three to five colors that are adjacent on the color wheel, such as red, red-orange, orange, yellow-orange, and yellow, or blue, blue-violet, and violet.

Anchor pin: A plastic four prolonged design mechanic that is attached to a container and holds floral foam industry.

Androdioecious: A sex form in deciduous species where staminate flowers on one plant and bisexual flowers on another plant of the same species are borne.

Androecious: A sex form in monoecious species where only staminate flowers are produced, giving rise supermale plant.

Androecium: Male reproductive component of a flower and its individual members are the stamens.

Androgenesis: The phenomenon where the male nucleus divides and give rise to a haploid embryo.

Androgenetic haploid: Plant having chromosomes from the male parent only.

Androgenetic: Genetic behaviour specific to the androecium, such as male sterility.

Andromonoecious: A sex from where staminate and hermaphrodite flowers are separately produced in the same plant.

Anemometer: An instrument by which wind speed is measured.

Anemone chrysanthemum: A group of chrysanthemum where the disc is raised as a result of well developed disc florets and the ray florets may be ligulate or tubular.

Anemone dahlia: Flower head with one or more rows of flat ray-florets surrounding a dense group of tubular disc florets look like a pin-cushion.

Anemophilous: Pollen transferred by the wind.

Aneuploid: An organism having a chromosome number which is not an exact multiple of the basic chromosome number (X) *i.e.* one somatic chromosome or chromosome pair may be missing or extra (2n+1, 2n-1, 2n+2, 2n-2 *etc.*).

Angiosperms (angiospermae): Flowering plants characterized by the presence of ovules in ovary and anther on a filament; two major subdivisions of angiosperms are dicotyledons and monocotyledons.

Annual mixed border: Similar to herbaceous border except that annuals of mixed flowers are planted in this type.

Annual rings: Cylinders of secondary xylem added to the stem of a woody plant in successive years.

Annuals: Annuals or seasonal are the group of plants which complete their life cycle (germination, vegetative growth, flowering, seeding and finally death of the plants) under a given site within one season or year.

Annulated root: Root having a series of ring-like swellings as in *ipecac.*

Antagonism: The phenomenon of one organism producing toxic metabolic products that kill, injure or inhibit the growth of some other organism in close proximity.

Anther Cap: In orchids, a cap of tissue that covers the clusters of pollen.

Anther culture: A method of micropropagation where the explant is immature pollen grains which produce either a small embryo by embryogenesis or a mass callus that may in turn undergo organogenesis to produce haploid plants.

Anther: Sac like structure of the stamen bearing the pollen grains.

Anthesis: The time of flower opening strictly, the time of expansion of a flower, but often used to designate the flowering period when pollen is shed from the anthers; the act of flowering.

Anthocyanins: A class of pigments (blue to red) found dissolved in the plant's cell sap, in contrast to flavones pigments occurring as minute particles or plastids, in the cytoplasm, the living layer within the plant cells.

Antibiosis: The adverse effect of feeding on a resistant host plant on the development and reproduction of the insect pest.

Antipodal cells: A group three cells at the chalazal end of embryo sac, *i.e.*, at the opposite end of the egg cell.

Antitranspirants: The chemicals which either partially close the stomata or form a thin film over the produce and check transpiration rendering to additional benefit in moisture conservation inside the plant, *e.g.*, mobileaf, kaolinite, phenylmercuric acetate (PMA), *etc.*

Apetalous: Flower without petals.

Apical bud: Terminal bud of a shoot, usually of the leading or main shoot.

Apical Dominance: The regulatory control of the terminal bud of a shoot in suppressing the development of lateral buds below it.

Apocarpous: When the carpels of an ovary are separate.

Apogamy: A form of apomixes where embryos develop form synergids or antipodal cells without fertilization.

Apomicts: Seedlings produced form seeds which have been developed as a result of apomixes.

Apomixis: Occurrence of asexual in place of sexual reproductive process where the embryo is produced from a cell in the embryo sac or surrounding nucellus which does not undergo meiosis but develop to form a zygote of the same genetic makeup as the female present.

Apospory: Type of apomixis in which the embryo develops from the integuments or nucellus.

Aquatic plant: Plant that grows in water. Three types of aquatics are – submergent: grows beneath the water surface, *e.g.*, water weed; Emergent: grows above the water, *e.g.*, water lilies; Floaters: floats on water surface, *e.g.*, water lettuce.

Arbor: A structure used for suspending vines. It is open in the center and covered by an open-latticed framework.

Arboretum (Arborium): An area set aside for the growing and effective display of all kinds of woody ornamental trees, shrubs, vines, and other plants.

Arboriculture: The art of cultivating trees primarily for shade or landscape effects.

Arborist: A person who has studied arboriculture and is qualified to make tree repairs and prune large shade trees.

Arbour system: Syn. Bower system.

Arc-and-Tangent Landscape style: It is a combination of all four curvilinear, radial, rectilinear and diagonal styles by using vertical, horizontal and 45 degree lines combined with arcs and circles to create a well organized and dynamic space.

Arch: Rectangular or semi-circular structure beautified with ornamental climbers which serves as a gateway.

Areole: A fore-shortened branch found on the stem of cactus from which spines and flowers arise.

Arm Bouquet: A grouping of flowers and foliages that is tied together and cradled in the bride's left arm.

Aroid: Any plant of the family Araceae that have small flowers massed on a spadix surrounded by a large spathe

Aroma: A pleasant, distinctive smell or fragrant of any substance which can be detected by nose only; plays an important role in the development of optimal eating quality in fruit due to synthesis of many volatile compounds (esters, alcohols, acids, aldehydes, ketones, *etc.*) during the ripening phase of fruits.

Aromatic plants: Plants having a typical aroma due to presence of organic compounds derived from benzene, *e.g., Citronella,* sandal wood, *etc.*

Articulate: Jointed, normally a joint on the parent plant from where natural separation may occur.

Arviculture: Crop science.

Asiatic Lilies: Bulb crop native to the Asian continent. They come in a wide range of colours, including yellow, white, red and orange. They are forced throughout the year.

Aspect: A position facing a particular direction. This term is used to describe the position in which plants may be grown; *e.g. Hydrangea petiolaris* is suitably grown against a wall with a northern aspect.

Astro-Turfing: It is a synthetic lawn popularly used in developed countries in roof gardens as well as in play grounds.

Asymmetrical balance: Asymmetrical balance is achieved by equal visual weight of non-equivalent forms, color, or texture on either side of an axis. This type of balance is informal and is usually achieved by masses of plants that appear to be the same in visual weight rather than total mass.

Atrium: A structure that provides lots of above light for plants. Commercial buildings often have their foyer as an atrium. Many homes have built in atriums.

Attractants: Flower parts or products which attract the pollinators, pollen, odor, nectar, perianth color, *etc.*

Auricles: Appendages that project from either side of the collar. Auricles are described as absent blunt or claw-like.

Auriculate: The base of the leaf blade or perianth segment possessing two rounded ear shaped lobes projecting beyond the general outline of the organ.

AutoCAD: It is a software application for 2D and 3D computer aided design (CAD) and drafting, available as desktop application. It is widely used by the architects, landscape designers and engineers.

Autogamy: Highly self-pollination where cross pollination is less than 5 percent.

Autonomic: Endogenous rhythmicity of alternations between developmental activity and slowing or cessation of growth which is hereditary.

Autotrophs: Organisms capable of manufacturing complex organic nutritive compounds from simple inorganic sources, *e.g.*, green plants.

Auxins: A category of plant growth regulator that can control rate of cell enlargement, retard abscission of young or mature fruit, stimulate ethylene synthesis in fruits, rooting in stem cutting, induce cambial division, inhibit lateral bud development, may also act as herbicide *e.g.*, Indole Acetic Acid (IAA), found in plant and synthetic compounds: napthaleneacetic acid (NAA), naphthaleneacetaınide (NAAm), B-napthoxyacetic acid (BNOA), indolebutyric acid (IBA), 2,4,5-trichlorophenoxy acetic acid (2,4-D), 2,4,5-tri iodobenzoic acid (TIBA), 2,4,5-trichlorophenoxy acetic acid (2,4,5-T), 2,4,5-trichlorophenoxy propeonic acid (2,4,5-TP).

Avenue: A wide road beautified with ornamental trees along their sides.

Axil: The junction between a leaf and a stem

Axillary: Situated in an axil.

Axill: The angle formed by the leaf, shoot, *etc.*

B

Baby Bonsai: Syn. Mame Bonsai.

Back bulb: A pseudobulb that has completed its growth cycle and become dormant. It serves as a storage organ and may bear a dormant bud. Under favorable conditions, this bud may develop into a new plant if the pseudo bulb is severed from the parent.

Back pruning: Cutting back of canes to one to two bud level for vegetative growth, practiced in grape.

Backcross: Cross of a hybrid to one of its parents and offspring of such cross are referred to as backcross generation.

Backcross-pedigree method: A breeding method where two to three backcrosses are made and thereafter the pedigree method is followed to advance the generations.

Backfill Soil: Topsoil dug out of a hole and used to fill it during seedling transplanting.

Balance: Balance influence the eye movement as lines and shapes have visual weight or visual magnetism. Equal weights can be balanced only when placed equidistantly from the centre. If the weights are unequal, the heavier must move towards the centre for making balance. Symmetrical or formal balance is achieved when identical elements are positioned equidistantly from the central axis. In making the balance with the plants, their form, color and texture are kept in view. Asymmetrical or informal balance creates the same amount of interest on both sides of the outdoor room, but does not create an exact duplication of elements. A tree on one side is balanced by planting a group of shrubs on the other side.

Balled and Burlapped: A tree or shrub seedling that is offered for sale with a ball of soil around its roots and wrapped in burlap.

Band placement: Application of fertilizer in bands to one or both sides of the seed or plant.

Band seeding: Placing the seed in rows directly above but not in contact with band of fertilizer.

Bandstand: It is a circular or semicircular structure set in a park, garden pier or indoor space, designated to accommodate musical bands performing concerts or orchestra to perform especially for various ceremonies and wedding functions.

Baradari: A canopied building with twelve doors situated at the upper most site of Mughal garden from where visitors enjoy the beauty of the garden.

Bare Root: A tree or shrub seedling that is offered for sale without soil around its roots.

Bark slipping: Active division of cambial cells to produce young thin-walled cells on each side of the cambium which separate readily (slip) from one another, leading to easy separation of bark from wood.

Bark: The part of the stem or root exterior to the vascular cambium.

Basal bud: Small leaf buds at the base of the blossom buds or at the base of young shoot.

Basal Cutting: A young shoot severed at the base of a plant, at or below ground level, and used for propagation. Dahlias and chrysanthemums are often propagated by basal cuttings.

Basal plate: The solid tissue at the bottom of a bulb to which the fleshy scales are attached.

Basal rooting: (Of a bulb) rooting only from the base, *e.g.* as in most European and American species of lily.

Base line: A line used as a base for further work, particularly in making a lay-out.

Base Plan: This important sheet details information such as site boundaries and other significant points of interest in regards to further development of the landscape or property.

Basic number: It is the genomic number (X) *i.e.*, the haploid chromosome number of diploid species or the haploid chromosome number of the ancestral diploid species of the polyploid species.

Basipetalous: In case of inflorescence where flowers open sequentially from apex to base.

Bastion: Bastions are projecting parts of ramparts and sections of certain types of fences used in landscaping.

Bearded: A petal bearing a tuft or row of long hairs.

Bed: Ridge of soil formed with furrows located on each side in which row crops are sown or transplants are planted for planting later in the field.

Bedding out: The cover of most or all of a bed or border with a temporary display.

Bedding Plant: A plant used for temporary display in the garden beds. Annuals and biennials raised almost to maturity and then bedded out often in large blocks for temporary display.

Belvedere: In Latin, belvedere means "beautiful view" and in landscape architecture, the term is used to indicate a structure such as an open gallery with a roof or a gazebo situated specifically to allow for a beautiful view of the surrounding area.

Bench mark: A point of reference in elevation surveys.

Bench terrace: A series of step like, mostly leveled platforms cut into hill slope for rendering cultivation in the sloping land.

Bent neck of rose: A physiological disorder causing bending of the stem just below the flower due to water imbalance, extreme temperature during transit, and lake of development of secondary thickening and lignifications of the vascular elements in the peduncle area subtending the flower head.

Bent-grass: Any of a genus (*Agrostis*) of grasses including important velvety or wiry pasture and lawn grasses.

Bents (soldiers): Grass stalks which have not been cut by the mower – flowering stems of perennial rye grass are the usual bents seen in a lawn. Remove by cutting off individually with shears.

Berm: A landscaping technique that is used to create interest, privacy, or screening. It may also divert water runoff. It is made by creating a mound of earth or a hill.

Bicolor: Having two clearly defined and sharply changing colours.

Biennial: A plant that completes its life cycle in two cropping seasons, the first involving vegetative growth and the second flowering and death.

Bigeneric: Plant arising from a cross between two genera.

Binomial Nomenclature: A system of naming plants whereby a plant is given a two part name representing the genus and species.

Bio-aesthetic Planning: (1) The planning of trees and plants with the object of beautifying the city roads, parks, public places and even the compounds of houses (2) A planned ecology of living beings from the artistic and aesthetic point of view in both rural and urban areas. Thus, it runs hand in hand with town planning *e.g.* Bangalore, the garden city.

Biocide: (1) A chemical which has a wide range of toxic properties, usually to members of both the plant and animal kingdoms. (2) A compound which kills.

Biological Control: The use of other organisms to control populations of pathogens.

Biomass: The total amount of living matters in a given area, expressed in terms of living or dry weight per unit area.

Biosphere: Part of the earth where living organisms exist naturally.

Biotechnology: The use of genetically modified organism and/or modern techniques and processes with biological systems for industrial production.

Biotic community: The plants and animals of a given habitat.

Biotic: Pertaining to living organisms in their ecological rather than physiological relations.

Biotype: Strains of a species of a pathogen, particularly an insect pest, differing in their ability to attack different varieties of the same host species

Biparous cyme: A cymose inflorescencen where two lateral axes develop at a time as seen in *Mirabilis jalapa, Carrisa karonda, etc.*

Bipinnate: Compound leaf which is twice pinnate *i.e.*, the midrib produces secondary axes bearing the leaflets, as in *Caesalpinia, Acacia, etc.*

Birch: A deciduous tree well suited for bonsai. The slender white trunk and Handsome form of the Japanese birch, *Betula japonica,* is attractive summer and winter. Several young plants grouped in a shallow container will form an enchanting grove with very little effort.

Bird baths: A small basin or trough fixed over a column for birds to drink or bath in it, constructed at a quiet corner of the garden.

Bivalent: A pair of sinapsed or associated homologous chromosomes during meiosis.

Blackout system: A means of covering plants to shorten the photoperiod, to promote flowering in short day plants such as *Chrysanthemum morifolium.* Black satin cloth or black polythene film is generally used.

Blade: The upper portion of the leaf. Often described as smooth or rough

Blanking: Floret sterility is in the flower head of the members of Compositae.

Blasting (Flower): The failure of bulb to produce a marketable flower after the floral initiation has taken place.

Blend: Seed consisting of a mixture of two or more cultivars of the same grass species.

Blind Bud: A bud that ceases to continue growth or fails to produce a flower, but remains vegetative.

Blind shoots: It is referred to some new branches of rose which just stop growing instead of going on to produce a flower bud after pruning.

Blindness (Flower): Failure of a bulb to initiate any floral part.

Blindness of gladiolus: The failure of a corm to produce any floral part.

Blueprints: This outdated term refers to the dark blue, white lined pieces of paper that were used by all types of architects, although not in the last four or five decades. Despite the lack of actual blueprints in landscaping projects per se, the term is still widely used by architects and contractors alike today.

Bluing: The objectionable development of blue pigment in flower petals, usually after harvest.

Bog garden: An artificial water garden used for growing plants which like their roots to be permanently wet. See also BOG PLANT.

Bog Plant: Plants which grow on marshy low land along the edge of the pond or lake, or plants that grow in boggy conditions and like their roots to be permanently wet. *Sagittaria sagittifolia*, water iris and rush are common examples of bog plants.

Bole: The main stem of a tree and somctimes only the lower part of the stem up to a point where the main branches are given off.

Bonsai: Bonsai is an art, which express in miniature the beauty of natural tree forms. The word 'Bonsai' is comprised of two words '*Bon*' means a tray or shallow container and '*sai*' means to grow; thus bonsai means something growing in a shallow container or tree in a pot.

Borders: It refers to the beds which are more in length than breadth and contains plants of heterogeneous characters.

Bosquet: A small group of trees, usually some distance from the house, designed as an ornamental backdrop in a French garden.

Botanical garden: An institution organized to maintain plant collections, usually representing a large number of genera and species to serve educational, aesthetic, scientific or economic purpose.

Botanical Insecticides: Natural materials obtained from plants that are toxic to the insect pest.

Botanical variety: A distinct morphological sub grouping within a species which may be recognized taxonomically.

Bottle gardens: It may be called as miniature greenhouse in which liliputian landscapes are planned. Any size of bottle, a jar, or a jug is suitable for gardening provided these are made of clear glass. Bottle gardening is a novel way of growing certain moisture-loving indoor plants, which may be otherwise impossible to grow in a dry house.

Bottle green: The art of making a miniature garden by growing delicate plants inside a bottle.

Bottom heat: Application of artificial heat to the rooting medium to keep the basal end of the cutting comparatively warm which helps in rooting.

Boulevard: A strip of land between two wide roads protected with low fence and beautified ornamental plants.

Bouquet: A flower bouquet is a collection of flowers in a creative arrangement. Flower bouquets can be arranged for the decor of homes or public buildings, or may be handheld. Handheld bouquets are classified by several different popular shapes and styles, including nosegay, crescent, and cascading bouquets. Flower bouquets are often given for special occasions such as birthdays or anniversaries. They are also used extensively in weddings. Bouquets arranged in vases or planters for home decor can be arranged in either traditional or modern styles.

Boutonnieres: These are worn by men on the left lapel of a suit coat or formal jacket and are usually compact. There are fewer variables to consider which makes their selection a little simpler. Color may match elements of the suit or his companion's garment.

Bower: A hut like structure with four open sides and beautiful ornamental climbers are trained on its roof.

Bract: It is a modified leaf subtending the inflorescence or the flowers. It may be scale like green, brown or highly coloured at the base.

Breeder seed: Seed, or vegetable propagating material, directly controlled by the originator (or in certain cases the sponsoring plant breeder or institution) and which provides the source for the initial and recurring increases of foundation seed.

Bridge graft: The insertion of a scion piece across an injured area of a plant by forming a graft union above and below the damaged tissue.

Broad leaf: A group of evergreen plants having large leaf lamina.

Broad leaved tree: A tree belonging to the botanical group called dicotyledons, and producing timber usually known as 'hardwood'.

Broadleaf evergreen: Plants that retain their green leave all year and possesss large leaves. Not needle bearing plants (conifers).

Broadleaf: Any plant with a flat leaf. Usually applied to evergreens (e.g azlea, boxwood, holly, rhododendron) with that sort of leaf rather than the needles found on pines, spruces, and firs.

Bromeliad tree: A synthesized tree planted with bromeliads. The shape of a bromeliad plant is not graceful and the colours are unimpressive, but when combined in a group on an uprooted trunk or driftwood, these plants appear elegant.

Bromliads: Monocotyledonous new world plants, robust in their growth and excellent for indoor and greenhouse decoration. With their colourful bracts and decorative foliage, they add elegance to any interior. They do not need much care and can survive in the shade for many months.

Browsing: Feeding on twigs or shoots, with or without attached leaves, of shrubs, trees or woody climbers.

Brushing: The use of a broom or broom like tool to clean the surface of the turf.

Buckhorning: Heavy pruning of a tree damaged by cold or being prepared for top working to leave stubs of large branches, which must be whitewashed, painted, or otherwise, protected to prevent sunburn.

Bud blasting of lily: A physiological disorder where buds stop developing and die prematurely during green house forcing due to insufficient light levels, too high or too low temperatures, prolonged vernalization treatment of bulbs and inadequate fertilization.

Bud drop: The loss of flower buds caused by stresses in growth or abnormal environmental conditions.

Bud necrosis: The condition of the floral bud where bud rots after abortion has taken place. This occurs due to poor ventilation, high temperatures and ethylene in the storage or due to attack of mites.

Bud notching: (1) Removing a notch of bark from the stem about 12 mm above the bud to assist the bud to make growth.(2) The removal of a wedge shaped piece of stem (*i.e.* bark together with a small piece of wood) directly above a bud to stimulate growth.

Bud opening solution: A solution containing floral preservatives like sugars, hormonal compounds and germicides used for opening of buds which are harvested at a stage earlier than that normally considered for harvesting

Bud opening: A method where flowers are harvested at a stage earlier than what is considered their 'cutting stage' and then opening them off plant. In this method the environmental conditions and chemicals used are identical to those used in pulsing but at a lower concentration.

Bud removal: Removal of buds in instances where growth is not wanted and would be almost certain to occur if they were retained.

Bud rubbing: The removal of blossom buds from their spurs by pushing or rubbing with the thumb and forefinger.

Bud scales: Protective scale like leaves of a bud during winter covered with hairs and impregnated with suberin.

Bud split: A disorder of *Lilium longiflorum* associated with aphids and high greenhouse temperatures.

Bud sport: (1) A branch, flower or fruit that differs genetically from the remainder of the plant, usually arising spontaneously. (2) A branch, flower or fruit that arises from a bud and differs genetically from the rest of plant. It is usually caused by a spontaneous mutation of cell genes. (3) A mutation in a section of a plant. Very often a single flower or a branch will differ in appearance from the bulk of the plant. If the section of the plant where the spot appears is propagated vegetative the mutation is perpetuated.

Bud union: Place of union of the bud with the plant stock in a budded plant. Should remain slightly above ground level while planting nursery plants in the field; if buried in the soil, scion roots may originate, and the budded tree may stand on its own roots after some time, which is not desirable.

Bud: A condensed young shoot in which internodes and leaves remain in a rudimentary or underdeveloped condition. Different kinds of bud include leaf bud, stem bud, flower bud and mixed bud.

Bud-burst: (of a bud stage) referring to the stage when the green leaves at the apex of a bud begin to separate.

Budding: A form of grafting in which the scion consists of a single vegetative bud.

Buffer: The use of landscape to curtail view, sound or dust with plants or earth berms, wall, or any such element.

Bulb Finger: An irritation resulting due to handling of tulip bulbs and cut flowers of *Alstroemeria*, *Narcissus* and *Tulip*.

Bulb Pan: A one-half sized 20 cm diameter pots used for forcing spring flowering bulbs.

Bulb Scales: These are leaf like parts of a bulb which are fleshy storage tissues surrounding the flower bud and are attached to the basal plate.

Bulb tunic: The dead, papery, leathery or fibrous covering that surrounds most bulbs.

Bulb Units: Referring to the annual increments of bulb growth especially in Narcissus.

Bulb: Bulb is a specialized underground organ consisting of a short, fleshy, usually vertical axis (base plate) bearing at its apex a growing point or flower primordial enclosed by thick fleshy scales. Bulbs are of two types: Tunicate and concentric: Amaryllis, daffodil, hyacinth, narcissus, nerine, tulip *etc.*, Non-tunicate and non-concentric: Lilium.

Bulbil: Diminutive bulbs (small and immature) are formed in the axils of the leaves or in the inflorescences.

Bulbing: The capability of a bulb or any other organ to form bulb or bulb like structures to behave as a bulb. A condition in tulips where bulbing has started but ceased at high temperatures is known as incomplete bulbing.

Bulblets: Miniature bulbs produced around the base of the mother bulb due to development of meristem in the axil of scale leaves.

Bulbous plant: Members of a group having bulbs, corms, tubers, tuberous roots and rhizomes and are grown commercially as cut flowers and flowering pot plants, *e.g.*, narcissus, daffodil, tulip, dutch iris, *etc.*

Bulkers: Those tulip cultivars producing small number of bulblets.

Bull head of rose: A disorder characterized by flowers having shorter stalks and a large number of petals than normal flowers due to thrips infestation, insufficient carbohydrate supply to developing buds and hard pruning.

Bull head: Spherically shaped flower bud usually resulting in to a malformed flower.

Bull-nose: A physiological disorder in daffodils where after reaching to the pencil or goose-neck stage of development, the flowers do not open properly.

Bush: A low woody plant, with a number of branches at or near the ground level.

Butt: Fruiting stem of a plant.

Buttress root: An asymmetrically thickened prop root, found at the base of certain trees.

Buttress: The flaring of a tree trunk near the soil. Most obvious in older specimen trees.

Bypassing shoot: Vegetative shoot develops immediately below the flower bud often occurring on azaleas.

C

Cabbage palm: *Livistona australis mart.* (*Corypha australis* R. Br.) A tall palm of family palmaceae, the young unfolded leaves of which are consumed as vegetable.

Cacti and succulents: Plants that thrive well without being watered for several days. Xerophytic in habit, these plants with their fleshy and showy vegetative bodies can withstand great heat and drought conditions. Cacti, with few exceptions, do not have true leaves and store water in roots and stems, white succulents retain water in the thick leaves as well. Grafting is possible with many exquisite combinations of cactus vs. Cactus or cactus over succulents.

Cactus dahlia: Fully double flower head of varying sizes with narrow and pointed tipped ray florets, *e.g.*, Arab queen, Eclipse, Lovely Looker, *etc.*

Cactus pads/Cactus paddles/Nopales: Edible cactus characterized by fleshy leaves. It is rich in vitamin C, some B vitamins, beta carotene.

Cactus: A plant having a fleshy stem, thickened epidermis,and leaves reduced to spines.

CAD (Computer Aided Design): CAD is simply, design and drafting with the aid of a computer. Design is creating a real product from an idea. Drafting is the production of the drawings that are used to document a design. Computer aided design (CAD) is the use of computer technology for the designs of objects, real or virtual. CAD is an important industrial art extensively used in industry and landscape architecture designing and many more. For landscape designs, CAD represents a practical solution for their imperative needs. CAD can be used to create 2D or 3D computer models. A CAD drawing is a file that consists of numeric data in binary form that will be saved onto a disk.

Calcareous soil: Soil containing sufficient calcium carbonate (often with magnesium carbonate) top effervesce visibly when treated with cold 0.1 N hydrochloric acid.

Callus: An irregular mass of undifferentiated parenchyma cells with various stages of lignifications which proliferate from cut tissues in response to wounding in normal condition. Callus are also induced artificially in tissue culture with the help of growth substances, vitamins, nutrients *etc.*

Calyx banding: Placing a rubber band or 6mm wide clear plastic tape is used around the calyx of the flowers which have just start opening. This operation is referred as 'Calyx banding'.

Calyx splitting: A physiological disorder in carnation where the sepals beneath the flowers are unable to form a cylindrical calyx tube which supports the base of the petals and the calyx splits either half or completely

Calyx: The outermost envelope of the floral whorl, and its respective leaves are called calyx.

Cambium: A thin plant tissue located between the bark (phloem) and the wood (Xylem).

Camellia: Because of its large flowers and foliage the popular tsubaki, or *Camellia japonica* is unsuited for bonsai. But among the other species, notably *C. sasanqua*, there is a wide variety of neat, small flowered plants quite perfect for dwarfing.

Campandeiform: Bell-shaped flower corolla.

Cane: A long, narrow pseudobulb, usually having many joints or nodes.

Canopy: The spread of branches and foliage of a plant.

Capitulum: A flower head that looks like a large single flower but consists of numerous sessile or sub-sessile small flowers clustered together on a disc.

Capsule: One or more-celled, dry, dehiscent, many-seeded fruit and dehiscence takes place either by valves or pores as the fruit of *Rhododendron* sp. *Hibiscus* sp.

Carbon Dioxide Fixation: A cyclical series of reactions in which Carbon Di Oxide is reduced to carbohydrate.

Carboy: A large and heavy glass vessel, originally designed for the storage of chemicals but now commonly used as a container for bottle gardens.

Carotenoids: A group of yellow, orange and orange-red fat-soluble pigments present in plant parts. These are either hydrocarbons or its derivatives and are composed of isoprene units. Carotenoids occur in different forms like carotene, lycopene, lutein, violaxanthin, neoxanthin, capsanthin, bixin, xanthophylls, *etc.*

Carpel: Female reproductive organ of flowering plants consisting of an ovary, style and stigma.

Carpet bedding: A group of low growing closely planted and colourful bedding plants in various designs.

Carrion flower: The flower which emits a carrion odour to attract certain pollinators like carrion flies and beetles.

Cascade bouquet: A bouquet with a full rounded central area and trailing line of flowers and foliages.

Cascade style bonsai: A style in which the trunk of the plant is trained to hang over the edge of the container as it hangs over the ledge of a mountain.

Cation exchange capacity: The base-exchange capacity or measure of the total exchangeable cations a soil can hold.

Catkin: A type of flower cluster, usually bearing only female (pistillate) flowers or only male (staminate) flowers.

Caudex: A trunk of a tree that bears of a leaves only at its apex as in palm and tree ferns or the swollen stem base of certain perennial plants from where new growths appear.

Caudicle: A slender stalk-like appendage of the pollinium or pollen mass.

Cell: Basic structural and physiological unit of plants and animals.

Centre of diversity: Areas where cultivated plant species and/or their wild relatives show much greater variation than anywhere in the rest of world.

Centre of origin: An area where the given plant species is believed to have originated realizing its greatest genetic diversity in that area.

Certified seed: It is the progeny of foundation or registered seed that is so handled as to maintain satisfactory genetic identity and purity and that has been approved and certified by the certifying agency. This category of seed is distributed to farmers for cultivation.

Cha-bana: Tea flowers; the flower arrangement in a tea house.

Chain of life in cut flowers: It is the application of improved loss-reduction biotechnology in growing, harvesting, handling, marketing of floral products and educating the consumers for caring these at home. It couples the grower, wholesaler, retailer and the consumer into a single chain.

Chalking: A condition where storage tissues of bulbs in tulips and calla lilies become chalky to touch and appearance being caused mostly due to falling of bulbs and where damage is extensive these may not develop properly.

Char Bagh Design: A garden in a quadrant pattern with water channels dividing it into four sections is called as Char Bagh Design.

Character: Morphological, anatomical or physiological feature of an organism which is a product of the genotype x environment interaction.

Chasmogamy: A built-in breeding mechanism where pollination follows opening of flowers which favours self-pollination as seen in tomato, brinjal, chilli *etc.*

Chelates: Metal containing organic compounds specially useful in supplying mineral nutrients to plants.

Chemotaxonomy: A method of classification of plants where the chemical constituents of plants are used in taxonomy.

Chiasma: The visible connection or cross over between nonsister chromatides of homologous chromosomes during and after diplotene of prophase – I at meiosis.

Chilling requirement: The requirement of plants for a specific period of dormancy below a particular temperature to initiate flowering.

Chimera: Mixture of genetically different tissues in the same part of a plant which may result from mutation, irregular meiosis, somatic crossing-over or artificial fusion of unlike tissues.

Chipping: Sectioning of a bulb for propagation in such a way that scales pieces remain attached to the basal plate so that new bulblets are formed between the scales.

Chlorophyll: The green colouring matter of the chloroplast which trap the energy of sun light for photosynthesis. Chemical composition is $C_{55}H_{72}0_5N_4Mg$ (Chlorophyll a), $C_{55}H_{70}0_6N_4Mg$ (Chlorophyll b).

Chlorosis: A condition in which a plant or part of plant turns greenish yellow due to poor chlorophyll development or the destruction of the chlorophyll resulting from a pathogen or mineral deficiency.

Chokkan style bonsai: In this style a single specimen is grown with a straight and upright stem.

Chromatid: Longitudinal half-chromosome produced by replication.

Chromatin: A complex between DNA, histones and other proteins, and chromosomal RNA which make the chromosomes.

Chromatography: The technique of separating and analyzing the components of mixture of liquids or gasses by selective adsorption in a column of powder (Cohema chromatography) or a strip of paper (Paper chromatography).

Chromoplasts: Variously colored plastids mostly present in petals and fruits, and the coloring matters associated with them are xanthophylls (yellow) and carotenes (orange red).

Chromosome aberration: A change in chromosome number from the diploid state, or a change in chromosome structure from the normal chromosome complement.

Chromosome banding: The staining of chromosomes following specific procedures which produce many dark and light zones along their lengths, and this pattern of banding is highly specific.

Chromosome: Thread like structures present in nucleus which show-distinct change in their morphology during cell division. They are deeply stained with some dyes, particularly with the Feulgen's reagent. Genes are located in chromosomes in a linear order.

Chu-kengai bonsai: See KENGAI BONSAI.

Cilindra: A gift of glass flute containing a flowering mini cymbidium orchids.

Cladding material: Transparent mounted on the walls and roof of a green house. These cladding materials may be both rigid and flexible.

Cladode: One or more short, green, cylindrical or sometimes flattened branches of limited growth develop from the node of the stem or branch in the axil of a scale leaf, as seen in asparagus.

Clasped to stone style bonsai: In this style a single tree is grown with its roots trained over a stone or some blocks of boiler ash.

Classification: The systematic method of arrangement of plant in categories according to some definite sequence, and categories in common use are Division, Class, Order, Family, Genus, Species and Variety.

Cleistogamy: A built in breeding mechanism where flowers remain closed at the time of pollination which favours self-pollination.

Climber roses: These roses have long stiffer stems, produce large flowers in small cluster; originated from a cross between hybrid tea and noissete roses, *e.g.*, Golden Shower, Delhi White Pearl, *etc.*

Climbers: Climbers are the group of plants which have weak stems and ability to climb up the support with the help of modified organs *viz*: Clingers, thorns, rootlets, linear, latex, tendrils, roots, prickles, weavers *etc.* These climb over walls, arches, pergolas, trellis, pillars, cascade, gates and topiary.

Cloche: Structure made of glass, plastic or horticultural fleece placed over a plant for protection or for forcing early crops.

Clonal selection: A breeding method of sexually propagated plants based on the selection of superior clones from a wide range of clones on visual observation of morphological traits.

Clonal variety: One clone or several closely similar clones propagated by a sexual means.

Clone: An individual or a group of individuals that develops asexually from cells or tissues of a single parent individual.

Cluster flowering: Production of flowers in multi-stemmed trusses or cluster composed of many stems.

Clustered bonsai: Type of bonsai where several branches are allowed to grow from ground level in a clustered manner.

Colchicines: A poisonous alkaloid obtained from seeds and bulb of the autumn crocus (*Colchicum autumnale*), having the property to cause chromosome doubling.

Cold chain: Low temperature environment through which produce from field can reach to consumer in a fresh form which starts from construction of cold storage in the producing centers, refrigerated ships for exporting them to foreign market and development of cold storage at retail shops.

Cold frame: An enclosed unheated covering frame used for growing and protecting young plants in early spring and for hardening off seedlings.

Cold spots: Pockets of low temperature in an enclosed area due to non uniform distribution of heat.

Cold-Hardiness: The ability of plant to survive the minimum temperature of the growing area.

Collages: Collage is derived from French word, "coller" and literally means glue. It is an artistic floral handiwork containing pieces of coloured papers, texts photographs, natural objects, in addition to dried flowers, leaves, roots, bark, *etc.*

Collar: The area on the outer side of the leaf where the blade and the sheath join. The collar is lighter in color than the sheath or leaf blade. The collar varies in size and shape among turfgrasses.

Collerette dahlia: Flowers are single, about 12-15 cm in diameter with an additional row of short petals around the disc florets which forms a collar structure, *e.g.*, Scarlet Queen, Aureline, *etc.*

Colour border: A herbaceous border plants with flowers of only one or two colours.

Colour break: A form of mutation in chrysanthemums that causes their colours to change.

Colour sport: Occurrence of differently coloured flower in an established cultivar due to genetic mutation of part or the whole plant.

Colour wheel: A diagram illustrating the various primary, secondary, and tertiary colours, with their respective tints and shades as they are applied to design.

Column: The central organ of the orchid flower, formed by the union of the stamens and pistils.

Columnar: A slender, upright plant form.

Commercial floriculture: Area of horticulture which includes the commercial production and distribution of cut flowers, flowering pot plants, foliage plants, and bedding plants.

Community pot: A pot in which seedlings or plantlets are first transferred before being potted or set out as individuals.

Complementary or Contrasting Colour Scheme: Complementary colors are those that are opposite each other on the color wheel. They tend to have high contrast between them. The most common sets are violet and yellow, red and green, and blue and orange.

Complete Fertilizer: A fertilizer formulation that supplies nitrogen, phosphorus and potassium.

Complete flower: Flower composed of a short axis or receptacle from which arise four sets of floral parts sepals, petals, stamens, and pistils.

Composite flower: (1) A flower actually consisting of many smaller flowers, having both ray and disc florets (as in chrysanthemums). (2) A grouping of many tiny flowers that gives the appearance of being a single blossom.

Compost: An organic soil amendment consisting of highly decomposed plant organic matter.

Compound inflorescence: Where the main axis is branched and the branches bear the flowers.

Compound leaf: A leaf consisting of two or more leaflets borne on the same leaf stalk.

Computer Aided or Assisted Design and Drafting (CADD): CADD is a design process used by landscape architects along with other professionals involving the use of computers and digitally enhanced images to create precise, detailed drawings for a project.

Concrete: It is non-purified form of essential oil obtained mostly by solvent extraction method. Concrete contains 45-55 per cent absolute.

Conditioning/Hardening: It is a process of restoring the turgidity of the cut flowers from water stress during storage and transport. It is achieved by treating the flowers with de-mineralized water supplemented with germicides and acidified with citric acid

Conifer: An evergreen gymnosperm belonging to the order coniferales bearing cones and generally needle-shaped or scale like leaves and producing timber which often called softwood, *e.g.*, pine, juniper, *etc.*

Conservatory: A structure, generally a green house in which plants are conserved or displayed during difficult season.

Container Nursery: A nursery where plants are raised in containers.

Container stock: Nursery plants grown entirely in containers rather than being dug from a field.

Continual Bloom Garden: A garden planted with a mixture of plant species that bloom in different seasons so that flowers occur all year round.

Contour line: A line connecting points on the land surface which have the same elevation.

Contrast or complementary colour scheme: In this two opposite colours like red-green, yellow-violet and blue-orange are arranged.

Controlled temperature forcing (CTF): Procedure for treating Easter lilies, in which non-precooked bulbs are potted, placed in a controlled temperature area at approximately 16°C for 2-4 weeks and, subsequently, cooled at 2°–7°C for 6-7 weeks prior to being placed in the greenhouse.

Convergent leaf: A leaf type where a number of more or less equally strong veins proceed from the base of the leaf blade to its apex in somewhat parallel direction as in water hyacinth, bamboo, *etc.*

Cool colours: Colours (hues) com-posed basically of blue and green tones.

Cool hues: Blue (and sometimes violet) and its tints, shades and tones.

Cool-season plant: A plant that grows best at daytime temperatures of between 15°-18°C.

Coppice shoot: A shoot arising from an adventitious bud at the base of a woody plant that has been cut near the ground level.

Coppicing: Periodical cutting-back of trees which are replaced naturally by undergrowth from suckers, *etc.*, practiced in timber crops.

Corm: An annual solid and swollen part of a stem which is bulb like underground structure having growing point at the apex and the basal plate below which forms the roots and all around the body it has rings as scars of the previous seasons leaves. Every ring has a prominent nod just opposite the buds of its adjoining rings and many invisible buds. Every part of the corm has regenerating capacity. Entire corm is covered with shredded tunic as dry leaf bases. This storage organ differs from a true bulb in being composed mainly of thickened stem and therefore it is solid. The important examples are *Acidanthera, Alocacia, Crocus, Freesia, Gladiolus, Tetonia* and *Tigridia.*

Cormel (Cormlets): A small corm developing from and around the new developing (daughter) corm which normally has a very tough and intact tunic. It is as senile as the corm and can develop the flowers similar to a corm under optimum conditions.

Cormule: Similar and smaller than corm but normally larger than the cormels, with shredded tunic developing 1-4 laterally on first nodes or terminally at first node on the cost of spike. No further spike development in case it is terminal.

Corolla: Second accessory member of the floral whorl, and its constituent leaves are called petals.

Corona: A crown of leafy outgrowth from inside the petals of some flowers which adds beauty to the flowers and thereby attracts insects for pollination as seen in passion flower, oleander *etc.*

Corsage: A flower or small arrangement of flowers worn by a person as a personal ornament. Typically worn by women on special occasions (as, at a ball or an anniversary celebration), a corsage may be worn pinned to the chest, or tied to the wrist. It is usually larger or more elaborate than a boutonniere.

Cosmetic pruning: Minor pruning of dead or spent flowers and think, weak or crossing shoots to keep a plant tidy and balanced in its overall shape.

Costa: A longitudinal vein expending along the anterior margin of the wing.

Cottage garden: A garden of a type supposedly typical of country cottages in the nineteenth and early to vegetables, herbs and informal borders of annual and biennial ornamental plants (*e.g.* hollyhocks, wallflowers and chrysanthemums).

Coupling phase: Linkage between dominant alleles of two or more genes.

Cracking: Leaf and scape crack disorder of tulip being caused due to ethylene or boron deficiency.

Creep perennial: A perennial plant that reproduces by both seed and asexual means (rhizomes, stolons, *etc.*)

Creepers: Those plants which are unable to climb vertically on their own because of their weak stems.

Crescent Bouquet: A variation of the cascade bouquet that is designed in a C shape.

Crescent: A geometric design resembling a C shape.

Crest: A ridge (comb like tuft of hairs or soft bristles) formed on the falls as in Iris, which is most commonly orange or yellow in colour.

Critical day length: the day length above which a plant will flower depending on whether the plant is a short or long day plant.

Critical period: The period or the stage of development in the life cycle of a crop when it is most sensitive to the deficiency of a production factor and at the same time most responsive to the correction of the deficiency.

Crock: Pieces of broken earthenware used in pots for drainage.

Crocus pot: A small fancy container having several apertures in the wells in which crocus bulbs are planted. The pots can also be used for other small plants such as aubretia, *etc.* larger sizes are available with more holes in the sides for planning with strawberries.

Crop competition: The tendency of the plants growing together to strive for the common resources of growth.

Crop ecology: The branch of plant ecology which deals specifically with the study of the inter-relation amongst crop plants and environment including management practices.

Crop tolerance: The degree or the ability of the crop to be treated with a chemical but not injured.

Crop yield index: A measure of comparision of the yields of the all crops on a given term with the average yield of these crops in the locality. The relationship is expressed in percentages.

Cropping index: Number of crops grown per annum on a given land areas x 100.

Cropping intensity (Cropping Index): A method of expressing the number of crops grown on the same piece of land, *e.g.*, a monocrop is given a value of 100, a double crop of 200, and inter-cropping between rows in a full stand of a base crop of 150.

Cropping pattern: Yearly sequence and spatial arrangements of crops and fallow, on a given area.

Cropping scheme: The plan according which crops are raised on individual plots of a farm with an object of getting the maximum returns from each crop without impairing fertility of the soil.

Crossing over: Exchange of homologous segments between non-sister chromatids of homologous chromosomes; takes place during pachytene.

Cross-pollinated annuals: Majority of the remaining annuals.

Crown bud: (1) A flower bud whose development has ceased. It sometimes develops the appearance of a crown. Generally this cessation of development breaks apical dominance, resulting in the development of side shoots. Crown buds may be caused by excessively low or high temperatures or in long night plants by a series of short nights while the flower bud is developing. (2) Vegetative buds or shoots forming around flower buds following unfavourable environmental growth condition (as with chrysanthemums).

Crown graft: A type of graft in which the scion is fixed into a vertical slit in the bark and sap wood of the stock. Also called a RIND GRAFT.

Crown suckering: The removal of unwanted shoots growth from the vine head and trunk while the shoots are still Young; often referred to as suckering.

Crowns: The unknown cause where bulbs produce many offsets due to loss of apical dominance hence the plant becomes bushy with many thin leaves bearing normally no flowers.

Cryptogams: Division of spore-bearing plants comprising ferns, fungi, *etc.* which are destitute of stamens, pistils and true seeds, but often reproduce as a result of sexual act.

Culm: The jointed stem of a grass which is usually hollow except at the nodes or joints.

Cultigen: Plant or group of plants known only in cultivation which presumed to have originated under domestication.

Cultivar: Botanical name for horticultural varieties

Curvilinear landscape style: In this style large flowing curves can lead the eye around the property with step by step unfolding interest along the line of movement and circulation.

Cushion plant: A small plant shaped as a cushion-like mound, *e.g.* many alpines and certain types of saxifrage. Also known as a cushion forming plant.

Cuspidate: Leaf narrowing towards the apex in the form of a spine as in date palm, pineapple, *etc.*

Cut back: (1) To prune a plant by removing the terminal ends of shoots or branches. (2) To reduce to the original number, size, *etc.*

Cut flowers: Flowers grown specifically to be cut and displayed in vases and for other uses.

Cut greens/Cut foliages: Plant species having delightful, magnificent and charming foliage find various uses in fresh and dried floral designs and floral ornaments such as bouquets, wreaths, interior decorations, *etc.* Leather leaf, podocarpous, asparagus, fern are common foliage.

Cuttage: Propagation by means of cuttings. The making and tending of cuttings.

Cuttings: A detached vegetative material from a plant used to produce a new plant.

cv: The abbreviation for cultivar (variety); cultivar is the most acceptable term used for a collection of plants with like characteristics currently in cultivation such as the marigold 'Naughty Marietta.' See CULTIVAR.

Cyathium: Inflorescence of plants as Poinsettia. Relatively inconspicuous but bears pistils, stamens, and nectary glands.

Cybrid: Hybrid cytoplasm resulting from protoplast fusion.

Cytogenetics: Study of chromosomes in relation to genetics.

Cytoplasmic-genetic male sterility: Cytoplasmic male sterility for which a restorer gene is available/known.

Cytoplasmic and genic male sterility: Sterility of pollen grains which is governed by the interaction between sterile cytoplasm and recessive gene.

Cytoplasmic male sterility: A type of male sterility conditioned by the cytoplasm rather than by nuclear genes, and transmitted only through female parent.

D

Dai: A wooden base used under a container for an Ikebana.

Daisy Hook Method: A wiring technique for daisies or asters for use in corsages or boutonnieres.

Day neutral plant: (1) A plant that does not respond to the relative lengths of light and darkness in the daily cycle. (2) A plant which will flower under day length.

Dead Heading: Removal of faded flowers for providing fresh look to the plants or to prevent seeding.

De-blossoming: The removal of individual flowers or flower trusses.

Decapitation: Method of pruning trees for rejuvenation in which most branches are severely pruned.

Deciduous: (1) Shedding its leaves each year and being without leaves during the winter or dormant season. (2) A term which describes those trees and shrubs which shed their leaves in the autumn.

Decline: Gradual deterioration of a plant as indicated by loss of vigour, poor growth and low productivity.

Decomposers: Microorganisms that break down organic matter.

Decorative dahlia: This is the most popular section producing fully double flowers which may be globular and sizes vary from 5 cm to 45 cm in diameter, the florets are slightly curved and broad, *e.g.*, Kenya, Croydon, Master Piece, Arabian Night, *etc.*

Decumbent: Reclining or lying on the ground, but with the end ascending.

De-Eying (Scooping): Removal of primary apical bud in caladium to promote more leaf development.

Defoliants: Substances that initiate leaves to fall.

Defoliation: A reduction in the normal amount of foliage due to insect or fungal attack or other injury or spraying; may be partial or complete (applies to leaves only).

Deforestation: Removal of the tree crop from a piece of land without the intention of reforestation.

Dehiscence: The method or process of opening of a seed pod or anther.

Dendron: In Greek compounds, signifying a tree.

De-Shooting in carnations: When the side shoots after pinching are 3-5 cm long then retain 3-5 shoots per plant in standard cultivars. When the side shoots after pinching are 3-5 cm long then retain 6-10 shoots per plant in spray cultivars.

De-shooting: Removing newly formed shoots to prevent their becoming branches. Often called "summer pruning."

Desiccant: A drying agent.

Desiccation: Drying out

Design: The determination of a character of an object to serve certain purpose known in advance is called as design.

Designed Landscape: A designed landscape is a site that appears to be completely natural but actually has both features and elements that were specifically planned, designed, and built under the direction of a landscape architect.

De-Suckering: Removal of new suckers from base of the plants.

Determinate: The concept of restricted potential whereby a plant or organ has a genetically limited size and cannot grow indefinitely.

Diagonal or rectilinear – 45 style: The shapes are created in the same way as the rectilinear style; however the diagonal lines are introduced mostly at 45 or 60 degree.

Dibbling: Sowing or planting propagating materials in holes made with a planting peg.

Dichogamy: A characteristic possessed by some plants, and also some varieties, in which the stamens mature and shed their pollen at a different time than their pistils are receptive.

Dichotomous: Type of branching where each axis bifurcates at the tip as seen in *pandanus, hyphaene, etc.*

Dicot: A type of angiosperm characterized by seeds with two seed leaves or cotyledons.

Differentiation: Physical and chemical changes associated with the development and/or specialization of an organism or cell.

Digitate: A compound leaf palmately arranged in which the leaflets arise from the same point at the apex of the petiole.

Dihapliod: Haploid derived from tetraploid, *i.e.*, monoploid for two distinct genomes.

Dihybrid: Plant that differs by two Paris of genes.

Dimorphic flower: The condition where styles of two lengths, long and short are borne in the flowers of same species as seen in the flowers of Rubiaceae, Labiatae, Verbenaceae, *etc.*

Dimorphism: Presenting two forms, as long and short growths or permanent and deciduous branches.

Dioecious: (1) A term applied to a unisexual plant or variety or to a species whose individual plants are unisexual. (2) Type of expression where plants produce staminate and pistillate flowers on separate plants.

Disbud: (1) To remove surplus buds and shoots from a plant in order to encourage an exhibition-size flower. This is often done to chrysanthemum and is sometimes referred to as 'SECURING THE BUD'. (2) To remove growth buds from young fruit trees in order to create a desired shape.

Disbudding in carnations: Disbudding is the removal of visible (5-10 mm diameter) undesirable buds. In standard cultivars terminal bud is retained and all the lateral buds are removed. In spray cultivars terminal bud is removed and lateral buds are retained.

Disbudding: (1) The remove of a portion of the flower buds on a plant for the purpose of producing larger blooms from those which remain. (2) The process of removing flowebuds from a plant stem, generally to improve the size of the remaining bud or buds. In most cases the terminal flower bud is retained and all of the lateral (side) flower buds are removed stems of plant such as the carnation and chrysanthemum.

Disbuds: A term synonymous with standard flowers. Stems having all lateral flower buds removed.

Disc floret: These florets are situated at the centre of a flower of Composite family which are tubular, usually shorter and contain both male and female reproductive parts.

Disc: The central part of the flower head (capitulum) of a composite plant made up of many tubular flowers or a fleshy (or raised) development of the torus within the calyx or within the corolla and stamens or composed of coalesced nectarines or staminodes and surrounding the pistil or the basal plate of a bulb or corm.

Dish gardens: The art of making a miniature garden by growing cacti and succulents in a dish. The size of the plants should be in proportion to the dimension of the dish or tray used. If plants in the dish gardens grow out of size, then pruning is essential to keep them at desired heights.

Disinfectant: An agent that kills or inactivates pathogens in the environment or on the surface of a plant or plant organ before infection takes place.

Disorders of Lilium: Leaf scorch (Due to deficiency of Mn, Al which occur at over dose of nitrate level and add lime @ 10 ton/ha), Bud blast (Due to storage of water at the top of plant, competition for nutrients, fluctuating carbohydrate level, low light intensity and high nitrate level), Puffy foliage (Due to frost injury and stunting of plants).

Display: The pleasing visual arrangement of flowers and products.

Dissemination: The spread of infections material (inoculums) from a diseased to a healthy plant by wind, water, man insects, animals, machinery, or other means.

Distance hybridization: Hybridization between individuals belonging to two different species of the same genus or of different genera.

Distichous: An arrangement of leaves and branches in which they appear first on one side of the axis, then the other, to form two ranks.

Distinct: Separated, not united with parts in the same series.

Diurnal cycle: The rate of photosynthesis, the rate of respiration and the amount of carbohydrates available for growth and development during any given 24 hours period.

Diurnal: Flower opening during the day and closing at night.

Division: The process of splitting up plants, roots and all that have began to get bound together. This will make several plants from one plant, and usually should be done to mature perennials every 3 to 4 years.

DNA: Deoxyribonucleic acid is the genetic material organisms inherit from the parents.

Domestication: The process of introducing plants from the wild in to cultivation under human supervision.

Dormancy: The failure of seeds, bulbs, buds or tubers to grow due to internal factors or unfavourable environment.

Dorsal: In orchids, the upper-most sepal of the flower.

Dot plant: A bulb grown singly or in a small group at the centre of a bedding scheme where it is large enough and bold enough to act as a focal point.

Double Cooling: A type of cooling where pre-cooled bulbs are planted and returned to cold storage.

Double dormancy: A condition in seeds resulting from a hard, water-impermeable seed coat and an embryo that requires after-ripening.

Double flowers: Flowers with more than the usual number of petals and/or style and stamens modified to petals.

Double Nose Bulb: A commercial bulb with two daughter bulbs and axial meristems with a common basal plate.

Double Potting: A method of enhancing the display of potted plants by placing the potted plant in a more decorative pot.

Double stem: A condition where single bulb produces two separate floral stalks as oftenly occurs in hyacinths.

Double transplanting: Seedlings of coffee, coconut, areca nut *etc.* pulled out from nursery and transplanted in a second nursery. After attaining the stage or planting season, this may be planted in main field.

Drawing: The graphical representation of an object is called drawing

Dried ornamentals: The charm of dried ornamentals can be maintained from few months to years with lesser cost if protected from the damage of high humidity, as in dried ornamentals the microbial activities in the aging process come to still.

Drip: A planned irrigation system where all necessary facilities have been installed for the efficient application of water directly the root zone of plants by means of applicators (orifices, emitters, porous tubing, perforated pipe, *etc.*) operated under low pressure. The applicators may be placed on or below the surface of the ground.

Dry matter: The substance in a plant or plant material remaining after over drying to a constant weight at a temperature slightly above the boiling point of water.

Dry spell: (1) A period, usually of not less than two weeks duration, during which no measurable rainfall occurs at a certain place or region. When extended into a month or more, a dry spell is considered a drought. (2) A period, of not less than four days, during which the daily maximum temperature remain at least 3 degrees to 4 degrees C above the normal maximum and the relative humidity continues below 50 per cent.

Dry storage: a method used for long term storage of flowers where it is graded, sealed in plastic bags or boxes to prevent the moisture loss

Dry wall: It refers to the gardens planted with different plants laid on a wall or walls. Plants growing in the crevices of the stones and hanging down the face of a dry wall look beautiful.

Dutch Flemish period: A style of floral design that featured large flamboyant arrangements and accessories.

Dwarf trees: Smaller than normal; smaller size is due to stock not lack of normal growth.

Dwarfing: The under development of a plant or plant organs. May be caused by any type of diseases agent under certain conditions, or by faulty nutrition.

E

Easel spray: A one sided sympathy flower arrangement placed on an easel.

Easel: A tripod like stand for holding sympathy flowers.

Eco farming: It is the potential for introducing mutually reinforcing ecological approaches to food production. It aims at the maintenance of soil chemically, biologically and physically way nature would do it left alone. Soil would then take proper care of plants growing on it. "Feed the soil, not the plant" is the watch word and slogan of ecological farming.

Ecological design: Ecological design is any form of design which minimizes a destructive impact on the land by integrating its components. The value of ecological design is often seen rather early on in a project as the landscape architect outlines ideas and plans to best utilize a space. Landscape architects may also contribute greatly toward the overall preparation of the initial master plans, supervise construction work, prepare impact assessments at varying intervals as well as conduct assessments and audits.

Ecological restoration: Ecological restoration, also called the practice of the discipline of "restoration ecology," is the recently developed study of restoring an ecosystem through active intervention. Beginning in the early to mid 1980s, ecological restoration involves a variety of professionals such as land managers, scientists, and laypeople, all working in tandem for the goal of restoring and repairing different types of damage.

Ecology: The study of living organisms in relation to environment and there effects upon one another. The major classes of environmental factors relate to climate, physiography, soil and associated organisms. Autecology is the study of the ecology of a single species. Synecology is the study of communities and associations of organisms.

Economic botany: The study of plants of importance to man especially plants as source of food, clothing, drugs, and products used in industry.

Ecosystem: First coined back in 1930 by British botanist Arthur Roy Clapham, the term ecosystem is used to indicate an environment's natural biological and physical elements. An ecosystem is comprised of animals, plants, and microorganisms, all of which function together interdependently within the environment's physical factors, or the habitat.

Eco-tourism: It means responsible travel to natural areas that conserves the environment and improves the well-being of local people.

Edge: Evergreen, low growing plants having same characteristics as for planting a hedge are grown to form an edge.

Edger: A tool used to trim the edges of a lawn. A typical form is a rigid semi-circular blade attached to a long handle.

Edging: (1) any of several materials used to form the edge of a lawn and prevent grass growing into flower beds and boarders. Nowadays, edging is usually a thin strip of metal or plastic, sunk into the ground so that a lawn mower can run over it easily. (2) Any of various plants used to form the edge of a border. Dwarf hedging used to be popular as edging but nowadays small flowering plants are more commonly used.

Effective bloom period: The length of time when a plant is in conspicuous bloom.

Egress: A way out, or exit.

Elements of design: The elements of composition are the visual qualities that people see and respond to when viewing a space.

Elements of effect: Elements in a landscape design that elicit a response by creating moods or feelings in the viewer.

Elevation: A contour line or notation of relative altitude, useful in plotting existing or proposed feature.

Emasculation: Artificial removal of predehiscent anthers from bisexual flower or male flowers from monoecious plant or male plants from a population of dioecious plants prior to pollination.

Embedded drying: Desiccants like silica gel, borax, sand saw dust and perlite are used for embedding plant materials. Desiccants are substance that will extract moisture from the flowers by absorption.

Embroidery: A very curling decorative pattern within a parterre, created with trimmed yew or box or made by cutting the pattern out of a lawn and filling it with colored gravel in a French garden.

Embryo culture: A type of *in vitro* technique where young embryos after their removal from developing seeds are grown on suitable culture media. It is useful in the recovery of hybrid plants from distant crosses, propagation of orchids, *etc.*

Embryo rescue: A technique employed when offspring of a cross is aborted. In this technique the embryos are excised from the seed and are nurtured on nutrient medium in a sterile test tube until they become a seedling that is strong enough to be planted in soil.

Embryo: A rudimentary state of a plant developed due to sexual or parthenocarpic reproduction, consisting of an axis and cotyledon.

Emphasis: Emphasis focuses the attention on one feature and keeps everything else secondary.

EMS: A chemical mutagen, chemically Ethylmethane sulphonate.

Endemic: Restricted to certain region or area with a limited distribution.

Endocarp: The inner of the wall of a fructified ovary.

Endodermis: A sheath composed of one or more layers of modified parenchymatopus cells, which enclosed certain fibrovascular bundles.

Endophyte: A plant which grows within the tissues of another plant.

Endosperm: A portion of the seeds of certain plants lying alongside the embryo and consisting of slightly differentiated parenchyma stocked with food materials.

English flower arrangement: Emphasis is given on mass flower arrangement and is primarily a form of art, so as to make the arrangement attractive as far as possible.

Enrichment items: Enrichment items are elements of the outdoor room which are not essential for making walls, ceiling or floor but, make the place more useable.

Entire: Leaves without any indentation or division.

Environmental impact: Environmental impact is the change to a site's natural resources, usually referring to some negative change to animal and or plant life that is caused by man. Many architectural landscaping projects require that an environmental impact study be conducted before the development of a site may commence.

Environmental inventory: Environmental inventory is the recording of a site's man-made and natural resources, including variables such as animal life, geological characteristics, vegetation, and also the impact of man's presence in the form of housing, highways and the deposit of hazardous waste.

Enzyme: A complex protein that speeds up a chemical reaction without being used up in the process.

Epicalyx: A series of small sepal-like bracts forming an outer calyx beneath the true calyx, as in okra, china rose *etc.*

Epicormic shoots: Shoots that develop from previously dormant buds under tree bark after being stimulated by external factors such as wounding.

Epicotyl: The part of the axis of an embryo above the region of attachment of the cotyledons.

Epicotyls: The portion of the embryo axis lying immediately above the cotyledons.

Epidermis: The outermost layer of cells on all parts of the primary body - stems, leaves, roots, flowers, fruits, and seeds - but absent from root tips and apical meristems.

Epigeous germination: A type of seed germination in which the cotyledons rise above the soil surface.

Epinasty: Revelation of more growth in upper surface of leaf than the lower one which causes curling of leaf.

Epipetalous: When the stamens adhere to the corolla wholly or partially by their filaments and anthers remaining free as in *Ixora, sunflower etc.*

Epiphyte: A plant that grows on another plant without deriving nutrition from the host.

Epiphytic orchids: Live on the bark of trees or on moss covered rocks, fixing themselves with their strong fasciculate roots. They take nourishment from fine particles of rain water or from the detritus that collects around the roots, contrary to the assumption of their drawing food from the host plant. These orchids can be successfully grown in hanging baskets. Important examples are *Aerides, Cattleya, Dendrobium, Epidendrum, Phalaenopsis, Rhynchostylis, Vanda, etc.*

Episepalous: On the sepals; standing before the sepals.

Epistatis: Interaction between two different genes (Non-allelomorphic) where expression of one gene is affected by another one.

Equitant: The conduplicate leaves overlapping inside each other in two ranks in a strongly compressed fan as in Iris or Gladiolus and in other members of Iridaceae.

Eskimo (ice) tulips: It is a forcing procedure in tulips which are planted late in the fall, rooted at 9°C and then frozen at -3°C until defrosted for summer or fall flowering.

Essential oils: Volatile oils having strong aromatic odour present in oil glands as transparent spots in the leaves of lemon, eucalyptus *etc.*, in the fruit skin of orange, lemon, *etc.*, in the petals of rose, jasmine, in the wood of sandal wood, *etc.*

Ethylene inhibitors: These are chemicals used to inhibit the activity of ethylene by producing ethylene forming enzymes

Ethylene: An ubiquitous, volatile hormone, synthesized in plant parts under stress and also induced in plant (*e.g.*, For floral initiation) by the application of auxins or certain growth inhibitors. It increases respiration rate, hastens fruit ripening, stimulate root initiation in cuttings, promotes abscission, stimulates floral initiation, inhibits elongation, breaks rest in buds and seeds, and inhibit lateral bud development. 2-chloroethyl phosphonic acid (Ethephon) is synthetic ethylene releasing compound.

Etiolation: Abnormal elongation of plant parts or plants in absence of light which results in chlorophyll degradation, more auxin accumulation, and presence of more undifferentiated parenchymatous cells in the etiolated site.

Euphilic blossom: The flower in which pollination is restricted to highly specialized, sometimes unique pollinators.

Evapotranspiration (ET): Total amount of water loss due to transpiration by a crop and evaporation from the surface of soil and vegetation during a specified time from a particular area; also called consumptive use.

Evergreen tree: Tree that remains green for most part of the year and sheds leaves slowly throughout the year.

Evergreen: Persistence of functional leaves until new set of leaves has appeared *i.e.*, never without green foliage.

Everlasting: A plant retaining its form or colour for a long time when dried, *e.g.* various members of the daisy family. Such a plant is known as an everlasting or an Immortelle.

Exotic: (GK. exotikos = foreign) Foreign plant or variety, *i.e.*, the plant of foreign origin.

Explant: Generic term for the living vegetative plant material extracted for tissue culturing on an appropriate medium.

Extine: The outer coat of a pollen grain.

Extrait: An extrait is an alcoholic solution of odorous part of pomade and is an intermediate product in the preparation of absolute.

Extrorse: Turned outward as extrose anther when grooved anther-face is directed towards petals.

Exudate: A substance (usually liquid) formed inside a plant and discharged from diseased or injured tissues. The presence of exudates often aids in diagnosis (*e.g.*, fire blight).

Eye catcher: In architecture, eye catchers are structures, usually ruins built artificially, that are used for the purpose of catching and guiding the eye of the viewer out and away from the immediate garden area and into a wider expanse such as countryside.

Eye: The bud of a sympodial orchid that will eventually develop into a new lead.

F

F1: The progeny obtained by crossing two different genotypes. The first generation from a cross.

F2: Progeny obtained by self fertilization of or intermating among F1 individuals.

Façade: A façade is the term used to describe the front of any building that has some type of architectural treatment.

Facultative Long and Short Night Plants: Plants that do not require a specific duration of dark period for a response to occur but will respond faster if the dark period is extended and shortened respectively.

False germination: An appearance of germination by a dead seed, due to the swelling of the embryo, as it taken up water.

Family or private area: This is also known as outdoor living area. The elements and features in this area vary enormously with the family and climate, but must fulfill the needs of the family. The main functions of this area are: Screening neighbors from viewing and hearing, Screening from wind and shading from sun, to provide comfort to the family members, to entertain personnel guests.

Family: A group of related plants or animals forming a category ranking above a genus and below an order and usually comprising from several to many genera.

Fan and pad cooling: A system for cooling greenhouses used during the warmer months of the year. Warm air expelled through exhaust fans in one wall is replaced by air entering through wet on the opposite wall. The entering air is cooled by the evaporation of water in the pad.

Fancy: A flower bred specially for its variegated blooms, *e.g.* exhibition carnations.

Fan-leaved palm: A palm whose leaves are not pinnate or divided to the midrib or rachis, *e.g., Licuala, Livistona, etc.*

Farm forestry: It is system of growing trees on the farm boundaries or in a suitable site in the farm which provides firewood, small timber, foliage for fodder and manure; trees act as windbreaks and reduce soil erosion.

Fasciated: Any plant organ that flattened enlarged and often disorganized and abnormal or sometimes tetra logical widening and flattening of the stem.

Fasciculated roots: Swollen tuberous roots which are developed in a cluster or fascicle at the base of the stem as in dahlia, asparagus, *etc.*

Fastigiate: All branches growing vertically, parallel to the main trunk.

Feather: A lateral shoot developed on the current year's extension growth. Also the term given to side shoots on the trunk of a young tree that has not been pruned.

Feathering: A condition occurring from late spring to harvest in lilies, where all or the part of the inner scales developing around daughter axis elongate faster than they are filled and project out in a pappery appearance of top of the bulb to in grain in confusion as if these are sprouting in summer.

Fecundity: The ability of flowers to produce seeds that will germinate.

Fencing: A device that fixes the boundary of the farm or garden and helps to stop the encroachment of the land and protection from wild animals and cattle.

Fermentation: The metabolic breakdown of an organic molecule in the absence of oxygen or with low levels of oxygen to produce end products such as ethanol and lactic acid.

Ferns: Dwarf ferns and selaginella-especially the resurrection plant, or iwahiba, *Selaginella lepidophylla*, and katahiba, *S. caulescens* - are sometimes grown as bonsai.

Fertigation: Application of fertilizers with irrigation water. Its applicability depends besides the method of irrigation used, on the type of soil and crop, the climatic conditions or water quality and the types of fertilizers available.

Fertility restorer: The line used for maintaining the cytoplasmic and genic male sterile line which is identical to the male sterile line with respect to nuclear genotype but dissimilar in cytoplasmic constitution.

Fertility: Ability of an organism to produce viable progeny.

Fertilization: Union of male and female gametes in sexual reproduction.

Fertilizer analysis: The proportions of nutrient elements supplied by a fertilizer formulation.

Fertilizer: An organic or inorganic material of natural or synthetic origin applied to the soil or plant to supply elements essential to plant growth and development.

Festoon: A festoon is created by using ribbons or garlands of leaves which are then suspended down between two distant points. A festoon may also be a painted sculpture, usually Corinthian in nature and often found adorning friezes.

Fete galante: First popularized by the French painter Jean-Antoine Watteau, fete galante is a style of painting depicting landscaping, most usually outdoor, social gatherings (fetes) showing people engaged in dance and conversation.

Fibre: Thread like tissues of plant origin consisting largely of cellulose together with little lignin and having sufficient toughness due to hardened and elongated sclerenchymatous cells.

Fibrous: Fiber-like; containing fibers or thread-like parts.

Field (water) capacity: The amount of water remaining in a soil after the soil layer has been saturated and the free (drainable) water has been allowed to drain away.

Field nursery: A term sometimes used for a temporary nursery formed in or adjoining the areas.

Field wrapping: Packaging or wrapping vegetables in the field at the time of harvest.

Filament: Anther bearing part of a stamen.

Filiform: Thread-like or hair-like that type of antenna with segments quite uniform in size.

Filler flowers: Small flowers that are used to fill space and provide textures colour, and depth within a design also called fillers.

Filler trees: Trees placed in between the permanent trees at time of planting. The filler trees are removed before they interfere with the permanent trees.

Fimbriate: Bordered with a fringe of slender processes usually derived from the lamina rather than attached as hairs. Normally applied to petals with fringed margins.

Finished grade: Grade accomplished after landscape features are installed and completed as shown on plan as proposed contours.

Fixative: An additive to potpourri to hold or fix the scent or fragrance for an extended period of time.

Fixative: In perfumery, it is a material which slows down the rate of evaporation of the more volatile materials in the perfume composition.

Flat bulbs: The shape (flat side and round side) of the daughter bulbs produced by a bulbous ornamental plant.

Flavonoids: These are 15-C compounds (C_6-C_3-C_6) consisting of the two aromatic rings linked by an aliphatic three carbon chain and often synthesized in the chloroplasts. The hydroxylation pattern and degree of polymerization of the C_6-C_3-C_6 unit result in different polyphenolic compounds. The major flavonoids are anthocyanins, flavonols and flavones.

Fleck: A small, white to translucent lesion (spot) visible through a leaf.

Flipper: A mild positive pressure due to hydrogen swelling inside that can result in swelling of the lid which can be brought down to its original position with finger pressure and lid remains in that place even after removal of finger pressure.

Floater-sinker: A method of separating healthy bulbs from those affected with basal rot which float with other debris.

Floating garden: A type of vegetable garden found in the lakes of Kashmir valley where vegetables are grown on a floating base prepared with some grass (*Typha*), compost and other organic matters.

Flora: Asssemblage of plants of a given area, usually arranged in a systematic manner.

Floral arrangement: The art or craft of arranging plant material (foliage, flowers, *etc.*) in a decorative manner.

Floral arranger: People with the training required to make and copy floral designs.

Floral biology: Study of flower in relation to its opening, dehiscence of anther, pollen viability, stigma receptivity, *etc.*

Floral bud split: Due to high temperature or aphid infestation a condition in lilies occurs in which floral buds split at the perianth seam during stage 3 of the green house phase.

Floral bud: Immature flower that consists of petals, stamens and pistil.

Floral craft: Forms of crafting in floriculture like art of cut floral arrangements, bouquet making, loose flower arrangements, hair adornments, dry flower articles, potpourris, *etc.*

Floral design: The art of organizing the design elements inherent in plant materials, containers and accessories according to the principles of design to attain a composition with the objectives of beauty, simplicity, harmony, suitability and expression.

Floral designer: Person considered to be more skilled than arranger in that he or she has the ability to create and design unique floral art.

Floral diagram: Diagram illustrating relative position and number of parts in each of the sets of plant parts comprising a flower.

Floral foam holder: A wedding mechanic with floral foam encased in a plastic age with handle.

Floral foam: A block of material with a high capacity for water absorption and retention that provides mechanical support for cut flowers in an arrangement.

Floral formula: An expression summarizing the information regarding the number and arrangement of floral parts in a floral diagram.

Floral induction: An unobservable preparatory step of flower development occurring prior to visible flower bud initiation.

Floral initiation: Initiation of floral primordium from a bud.

Floral pitcher: Different dried ornamental plant parts are artistically arranged in various silver or golden colour pitchers for central or corner table decorations like any kind of fresh floral arrangement.

Floral preservative: Chemical (many proprietary compounds and/or mixtures) added to water to extend the vase life of cut flowers.

Floral primordium: Very early stage of flower bud.

Floral tints: Translucent paints that allow some of the flower colour to show.

Flore: The aggregate of plants growing without cultivation in a country or district, or indigenous to a particular geological formation; as a desert flora.

Flore-pleno: Refers to flowers having abnormally high number of petals occurring in carnation, narcissus and tulips.

Floret: Small individual flowers of a dense inflorescence as in flowers of Compositae family.

Floribunda rose: A class of rose which bears more numbers of large flowers in cluster at a time; originated from a cross between Hybrid Tea and Polianthas, *e.g.*, Queen Elizabeth, Delhi Prince, *etc.*

Floricane: The flowering and fruiting stem, especially of the brambles (Rubus).

Floriculture: Floriculture is a branch of horticulture which deals with commercial growing, marketing and arranging flowers and ornamental plants, which includes annuals, biennials and perennials *viz.*, trees, shrubs, climbers and herbaceous perennials.

Floriculturist: A person involved in growing, improving and teaching ornamental horticulture is known as a Floriculturist.

Floriferous: Describing a plant that flowers freely.

Florigen: A term given to the so-called "flowering hormone", which has been hypothesized for decades but has not yet been isolated.

Florilegium: Originally a collection of flowers, now often a written anthology concerning plants.

Florist: A person dealing with the business of cut flowers, cut greens, loose flowers and floral products is known as a Florist.

Floristic composition. A complete list of plants forming a plant community.

Florula: Plants which grow in a small, confined habitat, for example a pond.

Flower arrangement: Arranging flowers is a kind of art and successful flower arranger is a born artist. But, one can become reasonably conversant with this art with proper training, a lot of patience and perseverance.

Flower bed: A prepared bed, especially one used for cultivation of ornamental flowering plants.

Flower bud development: Progressive change in flower bud, from transition to flowering.

Flower bud differentiation: Changes in the structure of a bud that leads to the development of buds containing flower parts.

Flower buds: Buds containing undeveloped flowers; also referred to as fruit buds.

Flower differentiation: Complete morphological development of the floral organs following initiation.

Flower head: An inflorescence, containing usually small or medium-size flower clustered together.

Flower induction: An unobservable, preparatory step that occurs prior to visible flower bud initiation.

Flower initiation: Visible organization of flower primodia (buds) at the stem apex.

Flower longevity/vase life/display life/shelf life: The period for which flowers or foliage remain in presentable form without losing its grade and quality is known as longevity, vase life, display life or shelf life. Shelf life is used mostly in case of loose flowers.

Flower: The reproductive structure of angiosperms consisting of stamens and/or carpels surrounded petals and sepals.

Flower-gatherer: Special secateurs designed to hold a flower after cutting it.

Flowering hormones: hormones which initiate the formation of floral primodia, or promote their development.

Flowering plants: Greenhouse crop plants grown in a pot and sold in the flowering state.

Flowering regulators: regulators which affect flowering.

Flowerpot: A container, typically the shape of a small bucket and with drainage holes in the base, in which to grow plants.

Flower-spike: A cylindrically-shaped flower head.

Fluorescence: Physical property of chlorophyll for which it appears deep green and blood red and reflected light, respectively.

Flush: The growth is produced during a short period.

Flute budding: A method of budding in which a patch of bark is removed leaving a narrow connection between the upper and lower parts of the stock; a bud patch of same size from the bud stick is removed and fitted to the stock and wrapped with polythene sheet.

Focal point: One of the elements of good landscape design which is an architectural feature focused as a centre of attraction.

Focalization: A landscape design principle that creates interest and accent for a particular arrangement.

Foliage: The collective leaves of a plant or plants.

Folly: A garden structure specifically built as a visual effect that's intended to fool the eye.

Forcing: The flowering of a bulb or plant before or after the usual season using artificial growing environments to stimulate those environments required in nature or the practice of hastening plants into flower before or after their natural time.

Fork hoe: A type of hand-cultivator with two or three prongs instead of the more usual blade.

Forkert budding: Budding method. A modification of shield budding in which the flap of the patch on the stock is not removed but is used to cover the bud; the flap is cut off at a later stage so that the bud may not dry out soon. Good success in mango.

Form flower: A flower with a unique shape that is used to provide a focal point in an arrangement *e.g.* orchid.

Form: Mass contained within extremities of growth is known as form or the three dimensional shape of the plant canopy.

Formal garden: A garden design having straight lines, regular squares, rectangles, circles or ovals with symmetry *i.e.* an exact duplication of plant material in the, form and colour. *e.g.*, TajMahal garden in Agra, Shalimar garden in Kashmir *etc.*

Formazan: In the tetrazolium test, living tissues of the seed changes the 2,3,5-triphenyl tetrazolium chloride to an insoluble red compound chemically known as formazan which impart red colour to seeds.

Formulation: The form in which a pesticide is sold for use.

Foundation block: A planting of fruit trees in which stock is maintained permanently under rigid control to be used as a primary source for 'true-to-type' stock and not as a direct source of propagating material itself.

Foundation seed: Seed produced form breeder seed. It is source of registered and certified seed.

Frame-working: Method of rejuvenating old fruit tree or of one variety for converting it into desirable variety; method of grafting employed to retain and refurnish the complete framework of the tree. Only super-fluous branches and thin branches at the top are removed, leaving the remaining framework intact in which the gifts are inserted at the required places. Many methods, of which stub-grafting and side-grafting are easy of adoption.

Fresh flowers: Flowers marketed subsequent to being cut from commercial crop.

Friable: A soil consistency term pertaining to the ease of crumbing of soils.

Frond: The leaf of a fern or a palm.

Fuki-nagashi bonsai: A bonsai imitating the effect of wind and weather representing a group of storm-bent tree growing atop a mountain range along the seacoast. Also called Wind Swept Bonsai

Full bloom: Blossoming most of the flowers in the plant at a period.

Fumigate: To expose an enclosed area, *e.g.* a greenhouse to poisonous fumes in order to destroy insects, pests or fungus growths.

Fungicides: Substances that prevent, destroy or inhibit the growth of fungi in crop plants.

G

Gamaopetalous: Petals united by their margins to form a tube like corolla.

Gametophyte: A stage in plant development consisting of more than one haploid cell. In grass to the 8 + celled embryo sack, and the three-celled tube before fertilization takes place.

Gametophytic polyembryony: A case of polyembryony where two or more embryo formed cells of the embryo sac or other non-somatic tissue.

Gamma-garden: An area subjected to gamma-irradiating for the purpose of irradiating the whole plants in different stages of growth and for varying durations.

Gamosepalous: Having sepals united by their margins.

Garden designer: A garden designer focuses on the design of small gardens and outdoor living areas. Garden designers may also be well versed in the art of historic conservation of gardens.

Garden room: Usually a casually furnished extension of the living room that is sunny and houses a large collection of plants with room for lounging.

Garden: Garden is a place for growing plants.

Garland: Flowers and foliages woven or fashioned in to a strand or a rope.

Gazebo: It is a small pavilion structure situated at an elevated place from where an aerial view of garden can be seen. It is a common feature in English garden.

Geitonogamy: Cross-pollination between two neighbouring flowers of the same plant found in monoecious plants and is genetically equal to self pollination.

Gene bank: Large collection of germplasms representing materials from various parts of the world.

Gene pool: Sum total of all the alleles present in the breeding members of a random mating population.

Gene sanctuary: An area within the centre of diversity of a particular plant species which is protected from human interference.

Gene: The unit of inheritance and structurally a segment of DNA, arranged linearly in the chromosomes which by interaction with the other genes and the environment control the development of a character.

Genetic advance (under selection): Improvement in the performance of selected lines over the original population.

Genetic change: Persistent changes in phenotype due to alteration of genes and such altered genes can be demonstrated by inheritance and segregation studies in subsequent generations.

Genetic code: The set of rules giving the correspondence between mRNA and amino acids in protein.

Genetic conservation: Conservation and storage of plant genetic resources *i.e.*, divergent types which is primarily a service to crop improvement.

Genetic diversity: Measurement of generalized distance between biological population which otherwise depict the genetic architecture of a population.

Genetic drift: Random change in gene frequency due to sampling, error *etc.* and it generally occurs in small population due to greater sampling variance.

Genetic emasculation: Use of genetic factors to make the male gamete non-functional in self and or cross-pollination.

Genetic engineering: Synchronous with recombinant DNA technology it is artificial manipulation or transfer of genes from one organism to another.

Genetic equilibrium: In a random mating population; the stage in which genotype frequencies do not change from one generation, to another. It has reference to one or more genes.

Genetic erosion: Gradual disappearance of various forms of a cultivated species and of its wild relatives.

Genetic load: The proportion by which the fitness of the optimum genotype is decreased by the presence of deleterious alleles in a random mating population.

Genetic makeup: A term to indicate the hereditary factors in a plant.

Genetic marker: An allele tracked during genetic study.

Genetic purity: Inherent quality of seed which implies the ability of the seed to transmit the desirable characteristics of parents to the next generations.

Genetic recombination: The production by crossing over of chromosomes with gene combinations that differ from those in the original chromosomes.

Genetic resource: Genetic reservoir or genetic variation which provides raw material for the breeder.

Genetic shift: Changes in the genetic make up of varieties bred for a particular environment if grown over a long period in areas outside their adaptation.

Genetic variability: A measure of variation in population that is due to genotype which can be studied by using different genetic parameters like, genotypic co-efficient of variation, heritability, genetic advance, *etc.*

Genetic vulnerability: The susceptibility of most of the cultivated varieties of a crop species to a disease, insect pest, or some other stress due to similarities in their genotypes; usually, due to the presence of one (generally more) common parents (s) in their ancestry.

Genetic wipe out: Massive losses from pest and disease spreading on an uniform variety. Genetic base of the crop should be broader with the help of genetic resources to check this genetic wipe out.

Genetics: A study of the mechanism of transmission of characters form parents to offspring, origin of variation and gene action.

Genome: All the chromosomes of a diploid species which do not pair at meiosis and are distinct from each other with respect to their gene content and often morphology constitute a genome, symbolized as '*X*' *i.e.*, the complete set of chromosomes which is inherited as a unit from one parent.

Genotype: The genetic constitution *i.e.* gene makeup of an organism.

Genotypic variance: Component of total variance due to genetic difference among the genotypes.

Genus: A category of classification between a family and a species which includes a group of structurally or phylogenetically related or isolated species.

Geophyte: A plant growing with stem or bulb (bulb, corms, rhizomes and tubers) below ground.

Geo-textile: Any permeable textile (natural or synthetic) used with foundation, soil, rock, earth or any other geotechnical engineering-related material as an integral part of a human made project, structure or system.

Geotropic Bending: Upward curvature of tips of spike flowers due to the lateral downward movement of the auxins when held horizontally on the ground surface.*e.g.* gladiolus, antirrhinum

Germicides: A germicide is any type of products or agents that are designed to kill and destroy germs and bacteria on the surface of different things. They are normally sold in form of liquids and powder.

Germplasm pool: An assemblage of genotypes which are sowed as a gene complex reservoir for all characters, particularly for resistance to pests and diseases, hardiness, adaptability, *etc.*

Germplasm: A collection of genotypes of an organism.

Gibberellic acid: Growth regulator causing stem elongation in plants

Gibberellins: A category of plant hormone which is a natural product of *Gibberella fugikuroi* (Fungus) and higher plants. It promotes seed germination, cell elongation in intact plants, help in breaking rest in dormant buds, prevent flower initiation, induce parthenocarpic fruit set and replace low temperature requirement for flower initiation in some biennial plants *e.g.*, GA_3 and GA_{4-7} are commercially available among about fifty that have been identified so far.

Girdling: The interruption of phloem transport by removing a ring of bark from the stem or process of constricting the periphery of a stem which blocks the downward translocation of carbohydrates, hormones, *etc.*

Glabrous: Smooth surface and free from hairs or outgrowth of any kind.

Glade: Surrounded completely by woods, glades are open, grassy areas.

Glaucous: Coated with a fine bloom mostly grey or blue green in colour being formed by the waxy coating of the foliage which may easily be rubbed off.

Glazing: A transparent material used to cover a greenhouse frame.

Glochid: Tiny barbed hairs found growing from the aerioles of cacti. The presence of barbs and their small size make them have penetrated the skin. Specimens of opuntia called rabbit ears owe their woolly appearance to glochids and a lack of spines.

Gluten: The nitrogenous part of the flower of wheat and other grains insoluble in water.

Glycerin drying (Glycerining): Glycerin preserves foliage by replacing the natural moisture present in the leaf with a substance that maintains the leaf form, texture and sometimes the colour. Fresh and fairly matured foliage is ideal for glycerining.

Glycolysis: A series of biochemical reactions in respiratory process in which hexose sugar is converted to pyruvic acid with net gain of two ATP molecules.

Glycophytes: Plants those are sensitive to a high salt-concentration in the soil.

Gnarled style bonsai: Style of bonsai in which the trunk is twisted near the ground once or twice to form a knob or a loop.

Gohon-yose bonsai: Syn. Yose Ue Bonsai.

Goose foot: Three or five paths or which spread outward from a single point in a French garden

Gothic: Most prevalent during the twelfth through the sixteenth centuries, Gothic is a style of ornamental architecture that was considered to be old fashioned and passé by as soon as the seventeenth century. Gothic architecture is characterized by ornate, often grotesque decoration and usually includes flying buttresses, pointed arches, and ribbed vaulting.

Grade: The slope or lay of the land as indicated by a related series of elevations.

Gradient: The degree of slope of a pipe invert or road or land surface. The gradient is a measure of the slope height as related to its base. The slope is expressed in terms of percentage or ratio.

Grading: The cutting and/or filling of earth to establish smooth finish contours for a landscape construction project. Grading facilitates good drainage and sculpts land to suit the intent of landscape design

Graft compatibility: The ability of scion and stock materials to accept each other and be joined as one.

Grafting *in situ:* Grafting of desired scion on the directly grown rootstock in the orchard in order to get more vigorous growth of the plant as the root-system of the stock is not disturbed.

Grafting knife: A single-bladed knife with wood, bone, or plastic handle; may be straight (nonfolding) or folding; the blade is longer and heavier than that of a budding knife and differs in the tip being curved down to the lower edge (*i.e.*, the cutting edge is straight instead of curved at the end).

Grafting wax: A pliable, sticky, water repellent material made of bees wax, resin, and tallow and applied to waterproof a graft junction.

Grafting: Art of joining two separate plant parts together so that by tissue regeneration they form a union and grow as one plant.

Gram-negative: Not staining by Gram's Method.

Grandiflorus: Comparatively large-flowered; used in botanical names.

Graphic language: The mode of communication through sketches is called graphic language.

Grasses: Plants that characteristically have joint stems, sheaths and narrow blades (leaves).

Grassiness (Degeneracy): A physiological malady in Narcissus where leaves are many but flowers only a few.

Grassiness in carnation: A physiological disorder in carnation which refers to failure of plants to produce flowers. This is a genetic disorder which varies from variety to variety. Removal and destruction of affected plants is the only way of correcting this disorder.

Gravitropism: A plants response to the force of gravity.

Green belt: A strip of vacant, recreational or farm land encircling a community intended to protect the community against intrusion of objectionable real property uses from adjacent communities or to provide for the community' orderly future expansion.

Green building: Green building also known as green construction refers to a structure using a process that is environmentally responsible and resource-efficient throughout a building's life-cycle from sitting to design, construction, operation, maintenance, renovation, and demolition.

Green manure: Plants purposely grown to be ploughed or mixed in to the soil to rot and add organic matter to the soil.

Green roof designer: Green roof designers specialize in the practice of designing elaborate roof gardens for the purpose of storm water management, sustainable architecture, evapo-transpirative cooling, habitat creation, or merely for aesthetic purposes.

Green rose: A rose at premature stage with the green sepals prominently enclosing the bud.

Green wall: A green wall may either be free standing or a part of a structure that is either completely or partially covered with some type of vegetation which may be grown with soil or some kind of inorganic growing medium. There are two types of green walls, green facades, which are made from climbing plants such as vines that grow directly on the wall, or living walls that are comprised of components like modular panels, plastic containers, an irrigation system, the growing medium, and of course, the vegetation

Greenhouse range: A collective term for two or more greenhouses at a single location belonging to the same owner.

Greenhouse technology: It is the technique of providing favourable environmental or growth conditions to the plants. In greenhouses, the growing environment is altered to suit the specific requirements of plants. It is rather used to protect plants from the adverse climatic conditions of light, temperature, humidity, CO_2 and air circulation for the best growth of plants to achieve maximum yield and best quality.

Greenhouse: A greenhouse is a covered structure which protects plants from vagaries of weather or environment *i.e,* wind, precipitation, excess solar radiation, temperature extremes and considerable attack of pests and diseases.

Gregarious flowering: General flowering within one or a few years over considerable areas of all or most of the individuals of certain species that do not flower annually, which in some cases is followed by the death of the plant as seen in the bamboos and *Strobilanthes, etc.*

Grex: A flock or group, applied collectively to the offspring of a given cross.

GRID: It is an unit of measurement drawn from the existing structure or a building around which landscaping is to be done, which helps to create a relationship of garden or its components with building.

Ground cover: A low growing plant that spreads and forms a mat like growth over an area.

Group planting: Planting a group of 3-4 trees or more at specified intervals instead of planting in avenue.

Growth inhibitors: A category of growth regulator which inhibits growth of shoots, block action of auxin, GA and cytokinins, sometimes stimulates fruit and leaf abscission and senescence, can substitute for chilling, delays bud break, and inhibits germination, *e.g.*, abscisic acid (ABA, Abscisin, Dormin), phaseic acid, 2-transphaseic acid and theaspirone are natural growth inhibitors and synthetic inhibitors are succinic acid-2, 2-dimethyl hydrazide (SADH, B-995), B-9, Alar, (2-chloroethyl) trimethyl ammonium chloride (CCC, Cycocel), B-hydroxy ethylyhydrazine (BOH), 1,2-dihydro-3, 6-pyridazinedione, Maleic hydrazide (MH), 2,4- dichlorobenzyltributylphosphonium chloride (Phosfon-D), ammonium (5-hydroxycarvacryl) trimethyl chloride piperidine carboxylate (Amo-1618), a-cyclopropyl-a-(p-methoxy phenyl)5-pyrimidinemethanol (Ancymidol).

Growth regulator: Any substance or physical factor, either external or internal that influences a growth process; in a more restricted sense, a substance that influences growth.

Growth: Growth is an irreversible increase in size which may or may not be accompanied by an increase in dry weight or in the amount of protoplasm. It is the sum total of all the metabolic activities and normally results from the excess of anabolism over catabolism. It refers to quantitative changes in the life cycle of plants. The examples of growth not accompanied by an increase in dry weight are (i) germinating seeds (ii) etiolated plants.

Grubbing: The complete removal of a tree.

Gulkhand: It is a rose petal jam which is prepared by mixing rose petals and sugars in the ratio of 1:2 and mashing and drying in the sun. It is a laxative and commonly used for flavouring and sweetening purpose.

Gulroghan/Gulroban: It is a by-product of rose prepared by maceration of rose flowers with warm sesame seed oil. This product gets ready by absorption of volatile oil of rose petals into any other vegetable oil like sesame, coconut, *etc.* It is used as hair oil, aromatheraphy for body massage, *etc.*

Gummosis: A disorder particularly of citrus and stone fruits due to mechanical injury and attack of fungi, insects, *etc.* resulting in copious exudation or deposition of gum on stems/or a condition where bulb scales exudes gummy substances normally due to ethylene exposure. This substance sometimes becomes hard.

Guttation: (1) Plant sap which appears as drops at the ends of leaves, usually on moist cool nights. It resembles dew and is confused with it. Guttation water contains nutrients which may favour fungal growth. (2) The exudation of water through the leaves via structure called hydathodes. Guttation occurs largely at night because of root pressure when litter or no transpiration is occurring.

Gymnosperms: Plants that bear seeds that are not within fruits (naked).

Gynandrium: The structure in the orchid flower which results from the fusion of the male and female portions of the flower.

Gynoecious: A sex form where only pistillate flowers are produced giving rise a super female plant.

Gynoecium: The females part of a flower. The carpels or pistils in a flower.

Gynomonoecious: A sex form where pistillate and hermaphrodite flowers are separately produced in the same plant.

Gynostemium: The reproductive organ of the orchids, the stamens and the pistil are condensed and form a consolidated complex body, is called the column or gynostemium.

H

Habit: The looks, appearance, general style or mode of growth; as an upright, open decumbent or strict habit.

Habitat: It is defined as the natural abode of plants which includes altitude, latitude, aspect, elevation, microclimate, soil and water.

Half hardy annuals: These need sowing under glass but are later planted out in beds or these annuals need nursery-raising under protected conditions and thereafter planted in open, *e.g.,* Antirrhinum, stock.

Half-shrub: A perennial plant, only lower half of which is woody.

Half-standard: A tree having a clear stem of 1.35 m on top of which the branching system develops; 90 cm in roses.

Halophytes: Plants tolerant to high soil salinity conditions.

Hanging basket plants: Plants grown in basket containers or hanging pots suspended from the ceiling to add colour to bare walls.

Hanging basket: Container, usually plastic, used for bedding plants, foliage plants, poinsettias, and other plant material, Usually suspended from supports in greenhouse, and used to suspend plants in the home or garden.

Hanken bonsai: A bonsai with gnarled and twisted trunk suggesting a tree growing on a storm-swept crag.

Hankon style bonsai: Syn. Gnarled style bonsai.

Haploid: An organism or cell having only one complete set of chromosomes.

Haplomorphic flower: Flower with open bow-like shape.

Hard landscape: Civil work component of landscape architecture such as pavement, walkways, roads, retaining walls, sculpture, street amenities, fountains and other built environment.

Hard pan: Hard and impermeable layer formed in the soil profile by accumulation of materials such as salts, clay, *etc.* which impedes drainage.

Hard paving: Surfacing that is either poured in place, later hardening, or is set into place as modular units.

Hard scaping: The installation of non-plants elements in the landscape.

Hard wood cutting: Cutting made from mature hard wood for propagation and done in Bougainvillea, *etc.*

Hardening off: Adaptation of plants to outdoor conditions by withholding water, lowering the temperature or altering the nutrient supply.

Hardening: It is a treatment given immediately after the harvesting of flowers by using water (preferably warm de- ionized water containing some germicide) to restore turgidity.

Hardy annuals: These annuals need no artificial aid their growth and flowering, which occur in open. *e.g.* digitalis, rudbeckia, *etc.*

Hardy plants: Plants that can withstand harsh temperature variations, pollution, dust, extreme soil conditions, and minimal water requirements and the likes. These plants have ability to remain dormant in such conditions and survive.

Harvest maturity: It is defined as a point of time in which a crop can be harvested and it will continue to grow and develop to reach maximum quality if necessary.

Hastate: Arrow shaped, in triangular fashion both downward lateral points and one upward.

H-bulb: Small bulblets of tulip located between the outer fleshy scale and tunic.

Heat island effect: The elevated temperature in the urban areas as compared to the rural, less developed areas is referred to as heat island effect.

Heavy climbers: Climbers with vigorous growth which require strong support like bower, pergola, *etc. e.g., Passiflora edulis, Quisqualis indica, etc.*

Hectare: In the metric system, a land measure equal to 10,000 square meters. One hectare is equivalent to 2.471 acres.

Hedge: Shrubs or small trees and planted at regular interval to form a thick continuous screen are called a hedge.

Heel cutting: Any stem cutting pulled away from the main shoot with a small strip of bark (heel) attached. The edges of the heel should be trimmed before being inserted into the soil. In some cases, cuttings with heels strike more easily than those cut clearly below a node.

Heel in: Storing young plants prior to planting by placing them in a trench and covering the root portions with soil.

Heliophytes: Sun loving plant species which require intense light for normal development.

Hemizygous: A diploid organism having only one copy of a particular gene present in the genome *e.g.*, males are hemizygous for genes on the X chromosome (Sex chromosome).

Herb: Plant which is erect, smaller in size and posseses soft stem. They are generally unbranched and branching if present are few in number.

Herbaceous border: The planting of annuals in the border of a plot in a definite pattern. The border may be single faced or double faced. In single faced border is made in front of a background and annuals are arranged on the basis of height *i.e.* tall-medium-dwarf. In double faced border tall annuals are planted in the centre, medium annuals on both sides of tall annuals followed by Dwarf annuals *i.e.* Dwarf-Medium-Tall-Medium-Dwarf. This border is created in the centre of the property area of garden and can be viewed from all sides, whereas single faced border is viewed from the front side only.

Herbaceous grafting: A method of grafting in which harbaceous plants are grafted for various purposes such as, studying virus transmission, stock-scion physiology, and grafting incompatibility.

Herbaceous perennials: Some non woody perennial plants with soft stems that cannot be included in the shrub group. They are termed as herbaceous perennials.

Herbaceous stem cutting: Cutting consisting of the terminal portion of stems of herbaceous plants; practiced in dahlia, chrysanthemum, *etc.*

Herbaceous: A plant not forming a persistent woody stem whether it is annual biennial or perennial die down in the end of growing season and reappear the following season.

Herbarium: (1) A collection of dried, pressed plants; also the room or building in which such a collection is kept. (2) A collection of plant specimens that have been taxonomically classified pressed dried and mounted on a sheet of herbarium paper.

Herbicides: Substances used for inhibiting growth of plants, plant parts, or to kill/ destroy the plants.

Heredity: Resemblance among individuals related by descent due to transmission of traits (*i.e.*, genes) from parents to offspring.

Heritability: The degree of phenotypic expression of a trait that is under genetic control.

Herkogamy: Spatial separation of anthers and stigma in a bisexual flower as seen in orchid, pansy, iris, *etc.*

Hermitage: In landscape architecture, a hermitage is a small, rustic garden building, suitable living quarters for a hermit, that is used as a place to contemplate the beauty of the surrounding nature

Heterosis: Superiority (or even inferiority) of the F_1 hybrid over the parents which is the combined expression of genetically, cytoplasmic and physiological factors and may be attributed to the stimulation resulting from interaction of different heritable factors of the parents in the F_1.

Heterostyly: Existence of styles of two different lengths (Long style and short filament and vice-versa) in a bisexual flower which prevents self-pollination.

Heterotrophs: Organisms which require a supply of organic material or food from its environment.

Hidden hunger: It implies to inadequate availability of a certain nutrient, which results in poor yields without affecting plant growth.

High visibility colours: Warm hues, light values and bright intensities which are very noticeable from a distance.

Hikae: Earth depicted in the Sogetsu School diagramme by a triangle.

Hilling: Earthing up in gladiolus and other crops

Hip: It is referred to rose fruit which is also sometimes called hip. It is rich in vitamin C.

Historic preservation: Historic preservation is a specialty of landscape architecture that has evolved over time to include the maintenance of a site in either its current condition or the preservation of a site's original, historic appearance. Or, the term may also refer to the conservation of a smaller site that is a part of a larger project.

Hi-tech floriculture: The technology which is ultra modern, less environment dependent and capital intensive having improved productivity with quality produce is hi-tech Floriculture.

Hogarth Curve: A geometric shape resembling a slim S.

Holding: A pre-shipment short-term treatment to cut flowers in which the flowers are placed in solution of sucrose (Concentration 20 per cent and above) for a period of 12-24 hours at 100 lux light intensity and at 20-27°C temperature which prolongs vaselife, promotes opening and improves the color and size of petals.

Holding-solution: A solution containing 0.5-2 per cent sugar, commercially sold for increasing the vase life of cut flowers.

Homogamy: The condition in which androecium and gynoecium in a flower mature at the same time, thus giving rise to self pollination.

Homologous chromosomes: Members of paired chromosomes in somatic cells which are similar in size, shape and supposedly in function, one being derived from the male parent and the other from the female parent.

Homozygous: The condition in which homologous chromosomes of an individual posses identical gene with respect to any given pair of alleles or series of allelomorphs.

Hooded: The part of the flower arched over or partially enclosed by another part of the flower.

Horizontal resistance: Partial resistance equally effective against all races of a pathogen.

Horizontal trimming: There may be many places in the lawn where the mower cannot reach –around the base of trees, under spreading shrubs and along fences and walls. Horizontal trimmer will be best choice to trim and leave the space between the grass and obstacles so that the mower can go over the edge of the turf.

Hormone: An organic compound other than sugars, amino acids, organic acids, *etc.* synthesized in one part of a plant in biologically very low concentration and translocated to another part where it cause physiological responses. Hormones are categorized into five groups: auxins, gibberellins, cytokinins, growth inhibitors and ethylene.

Horticulture: Science and art of cultivating, processing and marketing of fruits, vegetables, nuts and ornamental plants.

Hotbed: A bed of soil enclosed in transparent material and heated to provide a warm medium for germination of seeds or rooting of cuttings.

House plants: Plants able to grow in indoor condition, used for interior decoration *e.g., Diffenbachia, Dracaena, etc.*

Hue: Pure colour with no addition of black or white

Humectant: A material with a high water-attracting capacity. When added to other materials that lose water too readily, it retards loss of moisture and retains freshness. Humectants, are used in tobacco, cosmetics, and some foods to stabilize moisture content.

Hybrid cultivars: A group of plants grown from bed produced by cross-pollinating two or more parental breeding stock.

Hybrid tea rose: A group of best quality roses originating from a cross between hybrid perpetual and tea roses, having attractive size, color and fragrance, *e.g., Montezuma, Super Star, etc.*

Hybrid vigour: A phenomenon that occurs when the F1 offspring of an inbred cross has qualities superior to that of either parents.

Hydrocooling: The use of cold water to cool fruit. Ice water is showered over the fruit.

Hydrolysis: The breakdown of complex molecules to simpler ones resulting from the union of water with the compound.

Hydrophyte: Aquatic plants that are normally grown in water, *e.g., Nelumbium, Victoria amazonica, etc.*

Hydroponics: The culture of plants in which the root medium is exclusively water fortified with dissolved nutrients.

Hydro-seeding: It involves mixing seed, fiber mulch, and fertilizer together in a mixing tank. This mixture is then sprayed through a large hose and nozzle over the prepared seedbed.

Hydrotropism: It refers to changes in the position of organs caused by differences in the water content.

Hypanthodium: Type of inflorescence in which the fleshy receptacles form a hollow cavity with an apical opening guarded by scales, and the flowers are borne on the inner wall of the cavity as in banyan, peepal *etc.*

Hyperturea: A replica lightweight rock material created by equal amounts of dry cement, sand, perlite, peat moss, and water. This is made into troughs, planters, and rock all in the manner of looking old.

Hypobaric storage: (1) A new cold-storage principle in which atmospheric pressure is reduced. The subatmospheric pressure lowers respiration by reducing both oxygen and ethylene concentration in plant tissues. (2) Storage at less than atmospheric pressure for long-term holding of plant material.

Hypocotyls: Portion of the embryo axis lying immediately below the cotyledons.

Hypogeous germination: A type of seed germination in which the cotyledons remain below the soil surface.

Hypoglycemic: An abnormally small concentration of glucose in the circulating-blood, *i.e.* less than the minimum of the normal range.

Hypogynous: (1) A flower with a superior ovary; that is one attached to the stem above the place where the other flower parts are attached. (2) classification of a flower in which the sepals, petals, and stamens are attached to the receptacle below the ovary.

Hypogyny: The phenomenon in which the ovary occupies the highest position on the thalamus while the stamens, petals, and sepals are separately and successively inserted below the ovary as seen in Chinarose, Magnolia, *etc.*

Hyponasty: Increased growth of the lower surface of a plant part resulting in upward bending of the part as in young fern leaves.

Hysteranthous: Where leaves develop after the flowers *e.g.* football lily.

I

I-budding: Type of budding in which a rectangular or square shaped bud patch from the desired scion is inserted beneath the made up flaps of the stock by giving two transverse cuts and a central vertical cut to produce the figure 'I'.

Ideal cut flower: An ideal cut flower should remain fresh with respect to its colour, fragrance and appearance without loosing its grade for reasonable length of time.

Ideotype: A plant with its morphology ideally suited for getting maximum produce under a particular condition or set of conditions.

Ikada-buki style bonsai: A raft like bonsai in which a young, well-branched tree is planted horizontally in a container. The recumbent trunk is convered with soil and the branches which rise from it resemble in time a grove of individual trees.

Ikebana: Japanese art of flower arrangement. Literally it means "Living Flowers".

Ikenobo: This is the name of the first school of Ikebana literally meaning "hermitage by the Pond."

Imbricate: Leaves and bracts overlapping in a regular pattern sometimes even encircling the axis.

Imperfect flower: (1) Flowers in which either functionable stamens or pistils are present, but not both. (20) Lacks either male (stamens) or female (pistils) flower parts.

Imposed dormancy: A condition of the bulbs where these neither sprout nor develop due to imposed conditions of photoperiod, temperature, *etc.*

Impoverishment: Deterioration of the inherent fertility status of the soil.

Impregnation: A treatment given to the cut flowers that prevents the blockage of the water vessels in the stem by microbial growth and stem decay. It is done by treating the cut ends of the flower stems with chemicals like silver nitrate, cobalt or nickel chloride for 10 minutes.

***In vitro*:** A Latin word meaning 'in glass' which implies that biological process are made to occur outside the body of the organism in an artificial environment like glass.

***In vivo*:** A Latin word meaning 'in living' which implies that biological process is carried out in living organisms.

Inbred line: A nearly homozygous line developed by continued inbreeding, usually selfing, accompanied by selection.

Inbreeding depression: Loss in vigour due to inbreeding refers or agricultural chemicals that cannot be mixed or used together because of undesirable reactions.

Incompatibility: In sexual reproduction, it is the inability of the gametes to unite and form a fertilized egg that can grow to maturity, and in grafting, the inability of stock and scion to unite successfully to form a composite plant.

Incomplete flower: A group of plants whose flowers are either without a corolla or calyx (Incomplete), as in the family Euphorbiaceae, Urticaceae, *etc.*

Incurve: The center of a corner planting. It is the natural focus of attention and a logical place to use a specimen plant or other focal feature.

Incurved chrysanthemum: A group of chrysanthemum characterizes by ball shaped large flower in which florets are smooth, rounded or somewhat pointed at the tip and of sufficient length to form a inward graceful curve, *e.g.*, Eve Turner, Green Goddess, Snow Ball, *etc.*

Incurving chrysanthemum: A group of chrysanthemum in which petals are incurved loosely or irregularly, *e.g.*, Cossack, Freda Wilson *etc.*

Indexed plants: Plants that have been tested by pathological methods and found to be free of known pathogens. Plants may also be indexed for specific pathogen.

Indian rhododendron: *Melastoma malabathricum* L. An ornamental large shrup of family Melas-tomaceae, whose leaves are used for feeding silkworms and fruits are edible.

Indicator plant: (1) plant whose presence in a given area is a tip-off about changes that may be occurring in the area's soil or climatic conditions. (2) A plant that indicates, in general, and often in a specific, in general, and after in a specific manner, a deficiency of plant nutrient in the soil. (3) A native plant that indicates, in general, and often in a specific manner, the nature of soil conditions with regard to moisture and salinity. Dominant species are the most important indicates of such conditions.

Indole acetic acid: A decomposition product of tryptophan produced by bacteria and occurring in growing points of a plant, used as a hormone to promote plant growth, abbreviated as IAA.

Indoor garden: Garden made inside the house or room with appropriate plants for interior decoration.

Indoor gardening: Indoor gardening is the art of growing and arranging plants indoor or in the house for its best use for function and/or beauty.

Inert ingredients: Substances, other than the active ingredient, which constitute a pesticide formulation

Inert: (1) A material having no biological activity, such as diatomaceous earth, silica aerogels, magnesium oxide, aluminium oxide, activated charcoal cow-dung ash and soap stone. (2) Not having or showing active properties, especially not having any chemical action.

Infection: The establishment of parasite within a host.

Inflorescence: Word used by botanists to indicate the entire floral structure of a plant the manner in which it develops its flowers, and particularly the anatomical arrangement of its buds and blossoms.

Informal garden: A garden in which the materials are located without emphasis on regularity and symmetry.

Ingress: A way in, or entrance.

Inhibitor: Generally refers to chemical substance capable of preventing growth process.

Insecticides: Substances that prevent, inhibit, destroy, kill insects (belonging to Class *Insecta,* Phylum *arthropoda*).

Instant gardening: Producing an instant effect planting material, often flowering subjects purchased from nurseries or garden centers in containers. In this way the seasonal planting restrictions which apply to many plants can be largely over come.

Intangible: A quality denoting something that cannot be touches.

Integrated Pest Management (IPM): An approach to pest control which attempts to use all the best management methods available to keep pest populations below the economic or the aesthetic injury level with least damage to life and the environment.

Intensive cropping: Intensive land use by means of frequent succession cropping.

Inter generic hybridization: Hybridization between the plants belonging to two different genera.

Interior plantscaping: The use of plant materials to improve the appearance of the indoor environment.

Interior Scaping: The use of ornamental plants for functional and aesthetic purposes.

Intermediate chrysanthemum: The inner florets incurved and outer florets are refluxed and are intermediate in shape to refluxed and incurved.

Intermediate colours: *Syn*. Tertiary colours

International Federation of Landscape Architects (IFLA): An organization of professional landscape architects from several countries whose primary purpose is promoting the art of landscape planning and design

Internode splitting: A disorder in carnation where the internodes splits due to the deficiency of boron

Internode: The portion of the stem, cane or pseudobulb located between two nodes or joints.

Interspecific hybridization: Hybridization between plants belonging to two different species of a same genus.

Interstock: A piece of plant stem placed between the stock and scion, resulting in two graft unions. It is used to join two species that are incompatible with each other but not with the interstock.

Intervarietal hybridization: Hybridization between two varieties of the same kind.

Interveinal chlorosis: Yellowing of leaf tissue between the veins.

Intrageneric hybridization: Syn. Interspecific hybridization.

Intraspecific hybridization: Hybridization between two genotypes of the same species.

Introgressive hybridization: Hybridization followed by recrossing with the parental species in such a way that certain features of one species are transferred to the other species without impairment of taxonomic integrity.

Introse: Tinward as introse anther when grooved anther-face is directed towards centre of the flower *i.e.,* towards androecium.

Invasion: Growth or movement of an infectious agent into a plant and its establishment in it.

Invert: The low inside point of a pipe, culvert, or channel.

Involucre: A single, a pair or a ring of small bracts or leaves subtending a flower or inflorescence.

Involucres: A group of bracts at the base of an inflorescence, seen in sunflower, marigold, cosmos *etc.*

Irradiation: Exposure of biological materials to radiations, more particularly to mutagenic radiations.

Irregular flower: Some parts different from other parts in same series.

Irregular landscape style: The irregular style combines multidirectional lines on a square grid which is not restricted only to 45-degree or 60-degree lines. It is suitable to make for a very bold and complex space.

Ishi-tsuki bonsai: A bonsai with a stone style in which one or more trees are planted on top of a rough stone, either in a pocket of soil or with the bare roots simply clasping the stone and running down the sides into a container of soil below. The effect is highly realistic, suggesting a tree perched on a mountain crag or overhanging a rocky coast.

Island bed: A flowerbed set off on its own, usually surrounded by a lawn and with tall plants planted in the centre, shorter plants around the edge.

Isogamy: A type of sexual reproduction in which the male and female gametes involved in the reproduction are morphologically similar which is generally found in lower plants algae and fungi.

Isogenic: Having the same genetic constitution.

Isolation distance: The prevention of crossing among plant population by growing them in different locations far away in order to maintain the purity of the particular crop.

Isotope: Different forms of an element which have separate atomic weight but identical chemical properties.

Italian Renaissance Period: An early style of flower arranging that is considered the beginning of flower arranging in vases.

J

Japanese flower arrangement (Ikebana)/Eastern style flower arrangement: Emphasis is given on spiritual and religious background and only few flowers are used.

Japanese Influence: A style of floral design emphasizing space and significant placement of each type of plant material.

Jiyubana: 'Jiyubana' means free flowers, which can be arranged both in 'Moribana' or 'Nageire' styles of 'Ikebana'. Wood, metal or any other material may be used in addition to flowers.

Juniper: Junipers are evergreen trees that are very easy to train as bonsai and are recommended to the beginner. The most popular is the shimpaku, *Juniperus chinensis*, particularly the prostrate variety sargenti, *J. rigida,* the Mt. Hakone juniper, or nezu, is also highly prizes for its beautiful form and needle-like leaves.

Jushi: These are the fillers and supplementary lines indicated in the Sogetsu School diagramme by the symbol "T".

K

Kakemono: A scroll used as a wall hanging which could be a scene of any of the four seasons, religious paintings or Haikus. It is hung in combination with the flower arrangement.

Katate-mochi bonsai: Bonsai that can be carried in on hand. They are about 18-30 cm in height. With their smaller containers they are easily moved about and a place for them can be found on any window soil or small table indoors.

Keel: Innermost boat shaped and loosely connate petals of the flower of Papilionaceae family.

Keiki: A plantlet that grows high up on a cane, pseudobulb or flower stem. When it has developed sufficient roots system, it may be detached and grown separately.

Kengal bonsai: A bonsai with overhanging cliff style which represents trees rooted in a high crevice looking down a deep gorge. This style is often likened to a waterfall and classified as Sho-Kengai (little fall), Chukengai (medium fall), and Dai-Kengai (big fall).

Kensan: This is a pin holder used in a flat container to hold flowers and plant material in place.

Kerb: A concrete or stone edging along a pathway or road often constructed with a channel to guide the flow of storm water and thereby serving dual purpose.

Kernel: Whitish fleshy body visible on removing the testa of the seed which consist of embryo and endosperm.

Kingdom: The highest taxonomic category.

Knot garden: A very carefully planned garden of small dwarf shrubs or even herbs. Planned in a pattern and kept in order by constant pruning and trimming.

Knuckling: A tulip disorder where shoots develop in to bulb scales instead of usual upward growth.

Kokedama: It comes from Japan and it's a style of the Japanese bonsai. Literally translated, "koke" means moss and "dama" is "ball"- therefore moss balls. It originates from the Nearai bonsai style — the miniature tree is taken out of its container and displayed on a handmade pottery or pieces of wood. Kokedama is also called the "poor man's bonsai".

Kyokkuk style bonsai: Style of bonsai where a single trunk is twisted once or several times as it has struggled for its existence in the wild.

L

Labellum: The lowermost odd petal of orchid flower varying in shape, size and color from other two petals.

Lanceolate: Shaped like a lance-head *i.e.* wider in the middle and narrower towards the apex and base as the leaf shape of *Nerium, Bambusa, etc.*

Land race: Mixture of genotypes of an inbred crop locally adapted as a population.

Landscape architect: A professional who designs plans for the installation of plants and inanimate objects outdoors to fulfill aesthetic and functional purposes.

Landscape architecture: It is an art of arranging land and landscape for human use, convenience and enjoyment.

Landscape contractor: A landscape contractor is trained in the building or installation of landscapes and is usually hired by a landscape architect to work on a project.

Landscape design: It is the determination of a character of an object to serve certain purpose known in advance. The landscape design is aesthetic (attractive in appearance) or economic (utilitarian purpose).

Landscape designer: Much like garden designers, landscape designers work to design and create all different types of landscapes, performing many similar services, but they are not registered or licensed and do not hold the distinction and title of a landscape architect

Landscape Garden: It is a design with definite use of plants to serve certain aesthetic or utilitarian purpose. It is a manmade creation for ornamental or practical or both the uses.

Landscape Gardening: It is the planning and planting of outdoor space to secure the most desirable relationship between the landform architect and plants to best meet the human needs for beauty and function.

Landscape Manager: A landscape manager uses their knowledge of a natural environment for the purpose of advising those in charge of the development or maintenance of that landscape. Landscape managers are often employed by estate management companies, nature conservation and agricultural organizations, and in the worlds of forestry and horticulture

Landscape plan or design: It is the graphic presentation of a landscape by using a standard scale or AutoCAD software on a piece of paper for easy conceptualization and execution according to the specified measurements.

Landscape Planner: Landscape planners focus on the planning aspects of projects for urban, rural, and also coastal land use. Landscape planners create written statements, strategies, and policies, and do evaluations and assessments with some planners having specialized areas that they focus primarily on such as landscape archeology.

Landscape plants: Landscape plants are those plants which are grown with the objective of beautify our surroundings. In addition to this these plants must serve certain functional, architectural and engineering uses.

Landscape Scientist: Landscape scientists are skilled in areas such as botany, geomorphology, hydrology, and soil science and use them to address practical problems in landscaping. Landscape scientists may handle projects ranging from small site surveys to the complete ecological assessment of vast areas of land for management and planning purposes, and they may also report on a project's impact on a particular species of animal or plant life in a specific area.

Landscape: It is the appearance of that portion of land which the eye can comprehend at a single glance.

Landscaping: The design and alternation of a portion of land by use of planting material and land reconstructions is known as landscaping.

Language of flowers: The tradition of assigning meanings to flowers to convey messages which was initiated and became popular during the Victorian era.

Lanky: Spindly growth – a stem with a gaunt and sparse appearance.

Latent bud: An undeveloped bud that has been produced normally, which for various reasons will not develop further unless stimulated by some unusual circumstance.

Lath house: A propagation structure made up of bamboo stripes which provide outdoor shade and protect container grown plants from high temperatures and high light intensities to reduce moisture stress and decrease water requirements of plants.

Lawn: (1) A grass grown as a green carpet of a landscape and is the basic feature of any garden. (2) Any open ground about a house or other building grown to fine grasses and maintained in good turf, especially for its aesthetic value.

Layering: A method of vegetative propagation of plants usually with flexible limbs (shrubs, vines)in which roots are generated on the limb before being severed for planting as an independent plant.

Layout: Allocation of treatments to the plots in accordance with the conditions of the design.

LD_{50}: The milligrams of toxicant per kilogram body weight of an organism that is capable of killing 50 percent of the organism under the test conditions.

Lead: An immature vegetative growth on a sympodial orchid that will develop into flower-producing structure.

Leaf area index (LAI): The ratio of leaf area (One surface only) of a crop to the ground area on which it grows.

Leaf area ratio (LAR): The dry matter accumulation by the leaf in relation to its area.

Leaf Cutting: A whole leaf or part of one that is detached and used to raise a new plant.

Lenticel: Breathing pores in the young bark in the form of spots sometimes mistaken for disease very conspicuous in certain trees and shrubs as being coloured and of different texture.

Leucoplast: Colourless plastids that occur most commonly in the storage cells of roots, underground stems and other parts not exposed to light and it convert sugar into starch.

Liana: Very thick and woody, perennial climbers, commonly found in tropical forests *e.g., Hiptage madhablata, Bauhinia vahlii, etc.*

Light climbers: Climbers which are not vigorous in growth and can be grown easily on wire net *e.g., Bignonia purpurea, Clitoria ternatea, etc.*

Light intensity: The number of quanta or photons impinging on a given area.

Light pruning: (1) The method of pruning a trees or shrub by cutting back old growth moderately in early spring before the new growing season begins. (2) The removal of dead flowers from a plant.

Lignin: Strengthening material that occurs with cellulose and other polysaccharides in the middle lamella and primary and secondary cellwalls of higher plants.

Ligule: The structure which clasps the stem at the junction of blade and sheath. The type (membranous or hairy) and shape (tall, short, jagged, smooth) are distinguishing characteristics among turf grasses.

Lily pools: Water lilies and other floating plants such a *Pistia and Lemna spp.* Introduced into a garden pond to keep the water clean.

Limb neck of rose: A disorder causing bending of flower buds due to water stress or insufficient food supply to the flower buds.

Limber Neck (Stem topple, wet stem): Toppling of the floral stock just below the neck of the flower in certain Dutch irises, hyacinths, Lilium and tulips before or during flowering due to heavy flowers or imbalance of water or certain nutrients.

Liming: Application of lime in lawn field.

Limp neck: A disorder in rose caused by water stress in the area just below the flower head and the affected buds bend down due to the weight of the top.

Line Flower: A flower with a splice appearance *e.g.* Gladiolus, Snapdragon, Delphinium.

Line: One dimensional effect produced by arranging three dimensional objects in a certain fashion or the visual movement between two points within a design.

Lithophytes: A plant growing on rocks or stony soil deriving by deriving nourishments from the atmosphere.

Lithophytic orchids: Rarely found and they grow in moist, shaded rocks and crevices of walls. *e.g. Cymbidium munronianum, Diplomeris birsuta.*

Loam: A textural class name for soils having reasonably balanced amount of sand, silt, and clay. Loam soils can contain from 7 to 28 percent clay, 28 to 50 percent silt, and less than 52 percent sand.

Local variety: Unimproved plant types that is well adapted to a particular locality/ environment.

Locule: Compartment or cell of a pistil or anther. A descriptive term lacking precise morphological meaning.

Locus: The position at which a gene is located in a chromosome.

Lodging: Falling over, lying down, or broken over, as in plants beaten down by wind, rain, disease or insects, or combinations of these.

Long day plant: The plant which requires a day longer than its critical day length for flowering.

Loppers: A long handled shears operated with two hands and used for cutting larger branches.

Lux: The metric unit expressing the illumination falling on all points on a surface measuring one metre square, each point being one meter away from a standard light source of one candle 1 lux =0.093 foot-candles.

Lyrate: The shape of the leaf which is like that of a lyre *i.e.*, with a large terminal lobe and some smaller lateral lobe.

M

Macrame: Decoratively knotted rope or cord forming a harness-like structure for hanging pots.

Macronutrient: A chemical element that is required in large amounts (usually greater than 1 ppm) for the growth and development of plants.

Maiden tree. The first pruning is normally done when a tree is one year old and is called maiden tree.

Male sterility: Absence of functional pollen grains in an otherwise hermaphrodite flower.

Mame bonsai: Very dwarf bonsai plants not exceeding a height of 5-20 cm.

Margin: Edge of a leaf or petal

Marginal plant: Plants that will grow on the edges of ponds or lakes and when cultivated will make nice plants around a water garden, such as irises.

Marguerite carnation: Clove scented flowers of all shades of color with fringed petals, produce flower freely for a prolonged period but the flowers do not stand for a long time when cut.

Marker plant: A herbaceous plant that can be seen in the winter above ground and serves as a reminder of nearby plants which are not seen during the dormant period.

Mass arrangement: A design of many flowers, usually in a geometric shape that is based upon the lavish European flower arrangements of the 17th and 18th century.

Mass collection: Mass collection is the grouping of features based on similarities and then arranging the groups around a central space or feature.

Mass flower: A flower that is usually round shaped and is used most abundantly in an arrangement *e.g.* carnation, rose and aster.

Mass selection: Selection of a number of plants, heads or seeds phenotypically superior in characters from the population following their bulking for sowing in the next year and repeating this process till the desired improvement is achieved.

Master plan: Master plans are the preliminary plans outlining the proposed work to be done on a site. Because many projects are rather involved and therefore time consuming, master plans are subject to change throughout all the various phases.

Mat watering: Irrigation of potted plants by capillary. Mats are composed of fabric, cellulose or other water absorbing materials.

Mean sea level: The average height of the sea for all stages of the tide and at any particular place, it is derived by averaging the hourly tide heights over nineteen year period.

Meiosis: The process by which the chromatin materials are reduced qualitatively and quantitatively to half the somatic number of chromosomes which precede the formation of gametes.

Mentum: A chin like projection at the base of the labellum of orchid flower.

Mericlinal chimera: A type of chimera in which the mutated tissues occupy only a part of one of the layers and do not extend completely around the shoot.

Mericloning: Vegetative multiplication through meristem culture.

Meristem: A cell or region of specialized tissue whose principal function is to undergone cell division.

Mesophytes: Plants with characteristics intermediate between xerophytes and hydrophytes and are adapted where moisture and aeration conditions lie between both extremes.

Metaxenia: The direct effect of the pollen on the parts of a seed and fruit outside the embryo sac.

Micro flora: The multitude of microscopic organisms found in the soil. These organisms are responsible for the breakdown of soil organic material and the subsequent release of the nutrients. Certain micro flora will modify crumb structure.

Micro propagation: Production of plants from very small plant parts, tissues or cells aseptically in a test tube or other container where the environment, nutrition and hormonal balance are rigidly controlled. Enhancement of adventitious budding and then stimulation of root development from the base of the buds are accomplished in this propagation.

Micro-budding: Budding method similar to T-budding except that the bud piece is reduced to very small size, but it is not done in aseptic conditions.

Microclimate: Local climatic conditions near the ground or area around the plants resulting from the modifications of the general climatic conditions by local difference in relief, exposure, and cover, *etc.*

Micronutrient: A chemical element that is required in small amounts (usually less than 1 ppm) for the growth and development of plants.

Micropyle: Opening in an egg through which the sperm enters to effect fertilization.

Miniature garden: "Show-case" size garden where different garden features are designed in the miniature form.

Miniature rose: Type of rose whose leaves are small with little flowers borne on little bushes, useful for growing in pots and for edging rose beds. *e.g.*, coralin, pixie, *etc.*

Miniatures: Cut flowers consisting of several flowers supported on short, branched stems. Also known as non- disbuds.

Miticides/Acaricldes: Substances that prevent, inhibit, destroy, kill or mitigate mites (*Acarina arachnid* arthropods).

Mitosis: The process by which the nucleus is divided into two daughter nuclei following equational splitting of chromosomes *i.e.* nuclear division is preceded by DNA replication.

Mitsugsoku: A style of flower arrangement, which used a combination of candles (with a lamp-stand) and incense sticks (or burner) apart from the usual vase with flowers. Which are nothing but, respectively, deepadhar, dhupadhar, and puspadhar, the three essential items of worship according to the custom followed in India.

Mixed border: A border which generally beautified with herbaceous shrubs, sub-shrubs, herbaceous perennials, bulbous plant and annual flowers.

Mixed bud: Bud containing primordial tissue for both leaves and flowers.

Molluscicides: Prevent, repel, inhibit or destroy members of the Phylum *Mollusca* such as snails.

Monadelphous: Stamens fused by their filaments into a single bundle.

Monocarp: A plant (*e.g.* bromeliad, century plant) that lives for many years but flowers only once in a lifetime and then dies, new plants arising on the roots of the plant.

Monochasium: Type of inflorescence with a peduncle bearing a terminal flower with a lateral flower producing braches below it.

Monochromatic Colour Scheme: It is arranging different tones of the same colour either of the same species or in combination with different species. *e.g.* a yellow monochromatic colour scheme with variation in height is possible with yellow marigold, yellow antirrhinum, nasturtium, californian poppy and viola.

Monocot: A type of angiosperm characterized by seeds with only one seed leaf or cotyledon.

Monocotyledons: Plant herbaceous, less commonly woody, stems with vascular bundles not arranged in a single cylinder, leaves usually parallel veined, embryo with one cotyledon, *e.g.*, coconut, date palm, banana, pineapple, onion *etc.*

Monohybrid cross: When only one pair of contrasting character is taken into consideration at the time of hybridization.

Monohybrid: An individual heterozygous for one gene.

Monopetalous: One-petaled; all the petals united to form one body or organ, as a gamopetalous corolla.

Monoploid: An individual with the basic chromosome number (x), *i.e.*, with one genome.

Monopodial inflorescence: Type of inflorescence where the main stem continues to grow indefinitely by the terminal bud and give off branches laterally in acropetal succession.

Monopodial orchids: The plants grow upward with new leaves produced at the tip and flowers in the axils. They have neither rhizomes nor pseudobulbs. The important examples are *Habenaria, Phalaenopsis, Renanthera, Vanda, etc.*

Monotone: The use of one hue only but utilizing the full gamut of all its tints, shades and tones create a complementary harmony.

Moon garden: Garden developed in the tropical areas by using the ethereal value of moon light to linger at night where yellow or white flowering plants which show up well at night are planted.

Moribana: 'Moribana' means piled flowers, in which arrangements are made in shallow containers. The flowers and branches are supported with the help of pin holders, which are known as 'Kensan' in Japanese language. This arrangement looks very natural and is often called as natural 'Ikebana'.

Morimono: In this style fruits, vegetables and flowers are arranged and this style looks like 'English flower arrangement'.

Moringin: An alkaloid present in the root bark of sajna (Moringa sp.) which raises blood pressure, accelerates heart beat and constricts blood vessels.

Mosaic: A typical phenotypic variation in green and yellow tissue like a mosaic, caused either by "pattern" genes which continue to reproduce that pattern or by certain viruses rather than mutation.

Moss peat: A pure product containing over 75 per cent Sphagnum moss. When dry it is very light and able to absorb and retain moisture to 10 times its dry weight.

Mottling: Spots or blotches of different colour or shades of colour interspersed with the dominant color.

Mound: A small hill or bank of earth, developed as a characteristic feature in landscape.

Mound layering: Also called Stooling. Method commonly used in the propagation of apple root-stocks. Consists in cutting or heading back young plant in the nursery to 6 to 18 in. From ground, when new shoots develop from buds on the stump; earthing up shoots by heaping amount of soil around stump, which results in etiolation of covered portions, inducing them to throw out roots; then separating out the new rooted shoots from mother plant in the following dormant seasons, and transplanting in separate beds. Practised with apple, quince and pear root-stocks. Also called Stool Layering.

Mower: A machine mainly used for trimming grasses in the lawn.

Mowing: An operation consisting of trimming lawn grass at a certain height with the help of lawn mower.

Moyo-gi bonsai: A bonsai having free upright style in which the irregular upright growth is traditionally arranged in three tiers to represent heaven, earth, and man.

Multidimensional drawings: Renderings in 2D and 3D are often used to show various views of a landscape, allowing one to have a more realistic view of the end result. Features such as retaining walls, pools, ponds, and fountains are always easier to visualize if they're seen in their true three dimensional form.

Multifloral: Having more than one flower per inflorescence.

Mutagenesis: Induction of mutation by treatment with mutagens.

Mutagenic efficiency: Ratio of desirable changes free from associated undesirable changes or mutagenesis.

Mutant: An organism or cell showing mutant phenotype due to mutant allele of a gene.

Mutation breeding: Creation of mutants and if will for utilization in crop improvement.

Mutation: A sudden new variation in the genetic constitution due to individual gene or chromosomal changes.

Mutator gene: A gene which causes another gene or genes to undergo spontaneous mutation.

Mycorrhiza: Symbiotic association of a fungus in the root of certain plant species.

Nageire: 'Nageire' means thrown in and flowers are arranged in upright containers. Flowers must have sufficient stem length and these are supported with the help of cross bar fixture, which may be single or split types.

N

Naked flower: With no floral envelopes; without calyx and corolla.

NAP: The description of the lawn surface when all the grass foliage lies in the same direction.

Naphthalene acetic acid: It is a synthetic auxin plant hormone that is routinely used in the vegetative propagation of plants, in tissue culture of various plants and thinning of fruit apple.

Narrow leaf: A group of evergreen plants having needle like leaves.

Nastic movement: Movement exhibited by plants. The movement may be spontaneous such as the sleep movement of the clover (*Trifolium* spp.) prayer plant (*Maranta leuconeura*) and morning glory (*Ipomea* sp.) as they touch an object.

National park: An area owned by the state for the conservation of scenery, natural and historic objects of national significance and wild animals and plants by such means as to leave them unimpaired *e.g.*, Lucknow botanical garden, Kaziranga national park, *etc.*

Native plant: A plant that evolved naturally within a given geographical region.

Natural grade: Grade consisting of contours of unmodified natural land form.

Natural graft: A natural vegetative fusion of the tissues of contagious parts of different individuals, or sometimes of different individuals, or sometimes of different parts of the same individual.

Natural selection: An important features of certain theories of evolution and according to which, agents other than man determine which member of a population will survive. It refers of differential rate of reproduction of different genotypes of an organism in response to environmental factors.

Natural transition: Natural transition ensures that changes take place gradually for smooth and even look of the garden *e.g.* plant height or colour.

Naturalized Plant: A plant introduced from one environment into another in which the plant has become established and adapted to a given region by growing there for many generations.

Ncytophobic plant: Syn. Long day plant.

Ne-agari bonsai: A bonsai having roots above-ground style which characterizes bonsai whose roots rise high above the soil.

Necrosis: Death of tissue associated with discoloration and dehydration of all or parts of plant organ.

Need analysis: Need analysis is the compilation of an inventory of what should be accomplished by means of the landscaping and what the landscape will include, based on the preferences and life styles of the owner's family. To facilitate need analysis, the property area is divided into three areas as under: Public/Approach/Front area, Family/Private living area, Service/Utility area.

Negative geotropism: a post harvest disorder in gladiolus where the tips of the gladiolus spikes have the tendency to curve or bend down against the gravity if they are placed horizontally in transport

Nematicides: Chemicals that prevent, repel, inhibit or destroy members of the Class *Nematoda.*

Ne-tsuranari: Bonsai with connected root. The several trunks in the pots are offshoots from a single crawling root that lie exposed above ground.

Neuter flower: Flower without both androecium and gynoecium.

Niche: The role of an organism in the environment, its activities and relationship to the biotic environment.

Night-lighting: The installation of special lights to illuminate and beautify the landscape.

Nihon-yose bansai: See YOSE-UE BONSAI.

Nocturnal: Habit of flower opening at night.

Node: A joint or point on a stem at which leaves, flowers or other organs arise or have potential to arise.

Non tunicated bulb: A bulb without dry membranous outer scales. Such bulb is much more sensitive to drying more bruising.

Non-precooled bulbs (NP): Spring flowering bulbs not received precooling temperatures below 13°C before planting.

Nonresupinate: In orchids those plants whose flower lips are positioned uppermost relative to the inflorescence axis; the vast majority of orchid flowers are resupinate.

Nose: The tip of a bulb.

Notching: (1) A shallow cut into the wood just above a bud to force it into vegetative growth or just below a bud to promote fruit bud initiation. (2) Simplest way of planting a tree by just making a slit in the soil and inserting the roots; it provides very little soil cultivation.

Nucleoplasm: A dense but clear mass of protoplasm within the nuclear membrane.

Nucleus: A specialized spherical or ovoid protoplasmic body embedded in the cytoplasm of eukaryotic cell which is predominantly composed of nucleoprotein and responsible for growth and reproduction cell.

Nude flower: Flower without calyx and corolla.

Nurse crop: A companion crop which nourishes the main crop by way of nitrogen fixation and or adding the organic matter into the soil, *e.g.*, legumes intercropped with new plantation of fruit trees.

Nursery bed: A prepared area where seed is sown or into which transplants or cuttings are planted.

Nursery: Nursery is a place for growing plants before transplanting or rearing of plants before transplanting.

Nurseryman: A person, who propagates, grows, sells and sets out plants along with their care and maintenance.

Nutrient: Elements available from soil, air and water which are utilized by the plant for growth, development and reproduction.

Nyctinasty: A nastic movement induced by alternation of day and night *i.e.* light and darkness which otherwise called sleep movement as seen in leguminous plants, *Chenopodium, Gerbera, Portulaca, Carambola, etc.*

Nyctophilic plant: Syn. Short day plant.

O

Obake: A bicoloured type of anthurium popular for their two toned colourations, green and a major spathe colour.

Obcordate: Heart-shaped with a notch at the apex as seen in the leaves of *Bauhinia, Oxalis etc.*

Oblique style bonsai: Style of bonsai where plant is grown in an oblique position as if swept by wind and consequently having more branches on one side.

Offset: A lateral shoot or branch of shortened and rosette like appearance that originates from the base of the main stem as seen in date palm, and from leaf axil as seen in water hyacinth.

Offshoot: The generic term for adventitious shoot that arises from various parts of the plant.

Off-type: Any type of plant which is outside the acceptable limits of varietal variation.

Often-cross pollinated annuals: In many self pollinating species, cross pollination exceeds 5 per cent to 30 per cent and such species are referred to as often cross pollinating species. *e.g.* antirrhinum, linaria, larkspur, phlox, statice, lobelia, nemesia, pansy, viola, nigella and petunia.

Oligogenes: Genes having large individual effects; qualitative characters which show distinct classes are governed by these genes.

Oligophilic blossom: Flowers that are pollinated regularly by representatives of one major taxon of pollinator.

Ontogeny: The complete developmental history of an organism from egg, spore, bud, *etc.* due to the adult individual.

Open centre: A method of training trees where in the leader branch is pruned and diverging branches of approximately equal diameters at the base are developed leading to a spreading structure.

Open pollination: Pollination that occurs naturally, mostly implied to natural cross pollination.

Orbicular: Leaf blade more or less circular in outline as in lotus nasturtium, *etc.*

Order: A category of taxonomic classification ranking above the family and below the class.

Order: Order generally refers to the spatial layout or organization of the design and is most often achieved through balance.

Organelle: A specialized region in a cell that is bound by a membrane.

Oriental diamond: A fine packaging method for cut Cymbidium designed to add value to delicate flowers and used for special occasions

Ornamental bulbous plants: Those ornamental plants which have specialized modified underground stem structures to overcome the unfavourable environmental conditions are known as ornamental bulbous plants.

Ornamental garden: A loose general term for a garden designed for pleasure rather than utility, usually having formal flowerbeds separated by paths of grass verges.

Ornamental horticulture: The branch of horticulture that deals with the cultivation of plants for their aesthetic value.

Osmocote: Slow-release, encapsulated fertilizer.

Osmosis: The diffusion of water or other solvents through a differently permeable membrane from a region of higher concentration to a region of lower concentration.

Osmotic pressure: Pressure exerted by the water-absorbing property of a solution.

Osmunda fibre: The root moss of *Osmunda regalis* (royal fern) used in potting, particularly for certain epiphytic orchids and bromeliads.

Outdoor room: A landscape design concept which extends the indoor room outside by using plants to create walls and ceiling.

P

Paleobotany: The study of prehistoric plants.

Palmate: Having several (5-7 lobes, segments, *etc.* Spreading from the same point, like the fingers of the hand *e.g.* palmyra palm (*Borassus flabelifer*)

Palmatifid: Palmate but the segments reaching about half-way down as the leaves of passion flower *etc.*

Pan: A layer in the soil that is highly compacted or very high in clay content.

Panelling: Development of flat vertical dents, in large cans due to partial collapse of the body under high internal vacuum by over exhausting of cans which does not spoil the products but cans become unmarketable due to its appearance.

Panicle: Main axis of the raceme which is branched and the lateral branches bear the flowers as in *Delonix*.

Pankhuri: Dried rose petals which are made by drying the petals in shade and used in preparation of cool summer drinks and incense sticks.

Panynology: Study of pollen grains and other parts of flower belonging to the past geological ages.

Pappus: A tuft or whorls of delicate bristles or scales on the place of calyx as in certain Asteraceous plant.

Parasite: An organism that lives on or in another species and derives part or all of its nourishment from the living host.

Parenchyma: Tissue consisting of unspecialized thin walled cell, capable to divide.

Park: An open public place protected by low fence and several gates and beautifies with different plant materials statues, fountain, *etc.*

Parks and Recreation Planning: Landscape architects often work in parks and recreation planning creating protected areas in either their natural or semi-natural states for the purpose of recreational enjoyment. Parks and recreation planning may involve designing separate areas for certain activities while assigning others for rocks, water features, flora, and fauna. Some of the different types of parks and recreational areas planned and created by landscape architects include national parks, which are reserves of land usually owned by the government, urban parks, maintained by local governments, and private parks owned by businesses and or individuals.

Parkway: A parkway is a stretch of road laid through a garden or park style of landscape and usually contains a median strip along with plant life along the side of the road.

Parterre: A planting bed, usually square or rectangular, containing an ornamental design made with low closely clipped hedges, colored gravel, and sometimes flowers in a French garden. Parterres are usually laid out in geometric patterns, divided by gravel paths. They were intended to be seen from above from a house or terrace.

Parthenocarpy: Formation of seedless fruit from ovary without fertilization.

Parthenogenesis: The development of a new individual; from an egg (may be haploid or diploid) without fertilization.

Parts per million (ppm): Quantity of a substance contained in a million parts of a mixture or solution.

Pastoral: Pastoral is a term first used in the classical times of the Golden Age to describe the lowest level of formality, and in paintings, usually depicts the simple life of shepherds.

Patch budding: A method of budding in which a rectangular patch of bark is removed from rootstock and a bud shield of identical dimension is removed from the scion, placed on the stock and wrapped with polythene strip or adhesive tape; practiced in mulberry, walnut, rubber, *etc.*

Pathogenicity: The capability of a pathogen to cause disease.

Patio: A paved area adjoining a house, usually one that is the sheltered and adapted to sitting outdoors. The bareness of a patio may be relieved by plants in containers.

PCR: Polymerase Chain Reaction is a technique for amplifying a target DNA sequence.

Peat Moss: Widely used organic growing media component dug from peat bogs. Peat moss has light bulk density, good moisture holding ability, good air space qualities for the exchange of gases, adequate cation exchange capacity and a stable pH that is usually between 3.5 and 4.5.

Peat Pellets: Compressed peat moss disks used to start seeds or root cuttings and planted with the seedlings.

Pedicel: A stalk on which an individual blossom is borne.

Pedigree method: A method of handling the segregating generations which may be defined as a description of the ancestors of an individual where the hybrid progenies are maintained separately in the advance generations.

Pediment: A pediment is an architectural structure that is either triangular or segmental in shape and sits atop a door, porch, or window. Open pediments have an open center along the top portion while broken pediments have a part of the center of its base missing or open.

Peduncle: A primary flower stalk supporting either a solitary flower or cluster.

Peloric: In orchids; a term used to describe an unusual and often beautiful condition where all three petals (instead of just one) attempt to fashion themselves into lip colours and/or shapes.

Pendant: Hanging downwards or inclined.

Peony dahlia: Group of dahlia in which flower head consists of 2-3 rows of ray florets and a group of central disc-florets, the florets are usually broad, flat and somewhat irregular in form.

Percolation: Downward movement of water through the soil under gravity or hydrodynamic pressure or both under saturated or nearly saturated condition.

Perennial: A plant that grows year after year without replanting.

Perfect flower: Syn. Hermaphrodite flower.

Perfoliate: Having opposite leaves fusing together near the stem, so that in effect the stem, so that in effect the stem passes through the leaf. Leaves of this type are often found in honeysuckles and certain eucalyptus species.

Pergola: A pergola may be defined as a series of arches joined together. Pergolas are generally constructed over pathways, which add beauty to a landscape garden.

Perianth: The two floral envelopes considered together; commonly used for flowers in which there is usually no clear distinction between calyx and corolla, as the lilies.

Pericarp: Part of a fruit, developed from the wall of the ovary which may consists of epicarp, mesocarp and endocarp.

Pericycle: The layer of cells below the endodermis; the tissue from which branch roots originate.

Perigynous: The flowers in which the perianth and the stamens are basally united and borne on the margins of a cup shaped rim, itself being borne on the receptacle of a superior ovary neither above nor below it.

Perigyny: The condition where the thalamus grows upward the ovary in the form of a cup, carrying on its rim the sepals, petals and stamens and the ovary is said to be half-inferior as in rose, plum, peach, *etc.*

Peristyle: Peristyle literally means "surrounded by columns" and is a term often used to describe a temple-like structure that is enclosed within a colonnade.

Perlite: Lightweight, white growing media component originating from volcanic rock. Perlite is stable, sterile, has little cation exchange capacity has a pH of 7.5 and provides good water exchange drainage and aeration. Perlite contains fluorides that cause leaf damage to some monocotyledon plants.

Perpetual flowering carnation: Types of carnation which bear generally self-coloured flowers with serrated or fringed edged petals throughout the year.

Perpetual: The plants which continue to bloom more or less continually for whole of the year or most part of the year.

Personate: Forms of corolla in which the lips are placed so near to each other as to close the mouth of the corolla, as seen in snapdragon.

Perspective: Any object situated at a distance will look small compared to the one of the same size kept close to the vision is called perspective.

Pesticides: Chemicals or mixtures of chemicals that are used for killing. repelling, mitigating or reducing pest damage.

Pests: Organisms such as insects, rodents, nematodes, fungi, weeds, birds, bacteria, viruses, *etc.*, which damage the crops and reduce yield. Pests are injurious to human health and/or farmers economic efforts.

Petal: A modified leaf usually coloured and forms a part of a flower. This surrounds the stamens and ovaries and attracts pollinators.

Petaloid: Petal-like; sepals or stamens assuming the appearance of petals.

Phenophases: The stages of development in the life cycle of a plant in relation to the climatic condition.

Phenotype: The observed characters of an individual without reference to its genetic nature. So, individuals of the same phenotype may appear alike but may not breed alike.

Phloem: A tissue through which nutritive materials are translocated through the plant. The phloem consists of sieve tube cells, companion cells, phloem parenchyma and fibres.

Photomorphogenesis: A reaction in which the plant gets changed in growth and development in the visible light.

Photoperiodism: The response of a plant to non-uniform illumination, usually resulting in bending toward the strongest light.

Photorespiration: Light dependent O_2 uptake and conversion of photosynthates into CO_2 (Distinct from mitochondrial respiration). The C_4 plants photorespire at a much slower rate than do the C_3 plant. Therefore, less energy is wasted in C_4 while half the substrates are wasted in C_3 plants.

Photosynthesis: Biochemical reactions leading to synthesis of organic compounds, especially carbohydrates from the O_2 of water and carbon of CO_2 in presence of light as the source in chlorophyll containing tissues of plants.

Photosystem: A collective term for a specific functional aggregation of photosynthetic units.

Phototropism: The influence of light on the direction the different parts of a plant tend to grow (stems toward light, roots away from light). See also GEOTROPISM.

Phylloclade: A leaf-like or chlorophyll containing stem that performs the photosynthetic function of ordinary leaves as seen in *Opuntia, Euphorbia, Tirucalli, etc.*

Phyllode: Flattened petiole or any part of the rachis taking over the role of the leaf as seen in Australian Acacia, Parkinsonia, *etc.*

Phyllody: A disorder in which a much higher number of leaves than the normal are developed on a shoot in a rosette fashion.

Phyllotaxy: Arrangement of leaves on the stem or branch.

Phylogeny: Evolution of a race or genetically related group of organisms such as species, family or order.

Physical dormancy: Type of seed coat dormancy in which the seed coats and sometimes hardened sections of other seed coverings are impermeable to water, the embryo is quiescent (non dormant) but is sealed inside this water impermeable covering, seen in *Acacia, Albizia, Medicago, etc.*

Physical purity: Freedom of seed from inert matter, including broken seeds.

Physiological disorder: Disorders in which no primary parasite is involved and they are brought about by abnormal environmental conditions like, nutrition, weather, maturity, *etc.*

Physiological dormancy: A type of internal seed dormancy where the controlling mechanism apparently lie within the living, physiologically active seed covering, found in freshly harvested seed of many plants of the temperate zone which tends to disappear with dry storage.

Physiological maturity: The stage of development at which a plant or in grain crops the seed reaches maximum dry weight.

Phytochemicals: These are the secondary metabolites which impart taste, aroma, colour in food and has pharmaceutical and neutraceutical properties used in medicines and agriculture.

Phytochrome: A photo-morphogenic protein pigment in plants, involved in photoperiodic response of plants. It is present in two interconvertible forms: the red light absorbing form and far-red light absorbing form (pfr).

Picotee carnations: A group of carnations having narrow or broad rounded and smooth petals of yellow, white or buff back ground and bordered with a band of color at the margin.

Picotee: Petals with a narrow marginal zone of contrasting colour.

Picturesque: Picturesque is a term used in landscape architecture as well as in the world of art in general that is used to emphasize the artistic principle of conveying a number of emotions ranging from the commonplace to the colorfully surprising.

Pillowing: The technique of placing flowers close together and very low in a design, forming undulating peaks and valleys.

Pilose: Leaves or stems having long and soft hairs.

Pinch and half: First pinching is done in all the shoots when side shoots are 4-6 cm height then pinching is done in half of the shoots. This prolongs the flowering duration of plant.

Pinch plus pull pinch: First pinching is done in all the shoots and then keeps on pulling about 2-5 cm shoots so as to get a single large peak flowering.

Pinch pruning: Breaking by hand of the terminal bud.

Pinching: Removal of the terminal growing portion which reduces the height but promotes axillary branching, delays flowering and helps in breaking resetting.

Pinking: Unusual pink colouration of caladium leaves due to low temperatures.

Pinna: Leaflet of a pinnate leaf.

Pinnate: A compound leaf with the leaflets arranged on both sides of a common stalk. In bipinnate leaves the pinnate are divided into rachillae and petioles bearing pinnules. Also applied to feather like arranged veins.

Pinnatifid: When the incision of leaf margin is half way or nearly half-way down towards the mid-rib, as in poppy.

Pistil: The female reproductive organ consisting of ovary, ovules, style and stigma.

Pistillate: Presence of only pistils in the flower. Pistil -the female reproductive organ of a flower consisting of the stigma, style and ovary.

Pith: Central core of the stem and the root, usually made of large celled parenchyma with abundant intercellular spaces.

Placenta: The ridge of tissue in the inner wall of the ovary bearing one or more ovules.

Plant anatomy: The study of the structure of cells, tissues and tissue systems.

Plant chimera: A plant is said to be a chimera when cells of more than one genotype are found growing adjacent in the meristem, organ or tissues of that plant and its basic concept has developed from variegated plants.

Plant density: Number of plants per unit area in a crop field or flower field.

Plant Guard: The protection constructed around a tree to deter vandalism and help to prevent damage. It could be made of metal, bamboo or concrete or the like.

Plant introduction: An important step in plant breeding in which a genotype is taken into new environments where it has not been grown before.

Plant lifting: Removal of plants from nursery bed with or without earth ball for sale, replanting, *etc.*

Plant murals: A special kind of planter, which is like a wall plaque with herbaceous perennial growing vertically on the wall like a picture. It is just a hanging patch of green plants on the wall. It is ideal to other neglected place in the house.

Plant Quarantine: The use of legislation to control the import and export of plants or plant materials to prevent the spread of plant pest and diseases.

Plant shredder: Similar to a soil shredder but with heavier knives to tear limbs, leaves, and other plant debris into small pieces; usually trailer-mounted and equipped with a blower and chute to convey chopped up material into a dump truck or into a pile.

Plant vase: A nontechnical term that describes the rosette of leaves that ascent forming a cup at the base of the plant. It is common to many genera within the Bromeliaceae family.

Planter: Any container designed to provide suitable conditions for plant growth.

Planting: Planting is the operation of transferring young plant from nursery to their permanent place in landscape.

Planting board: A wooden equipment with three notches which ensures the planting in the correct position.

Planting box: A box or tray in which small plants are raised and transported to the field for planting out.

Planting out: Transferring nursery stock to the planting site as contrasted to transplanting in nursery.

Planting plan: A drawing specifying by means of symbols the types and names of plant species the quantities and their locations in a landscape.

Planting ratio: The male and female plants when planted in a certain proportion to ensure proper pollination and fertilization *e.g.*, 10:1 (Female: male) ratio in pointed ground.

Plantlet: Small, immature plant.

Plasma gene: A gene located in cytoplasmic organelle like-plastid, mitochondria which is responsible for cytoplasmic inheritance.

Plasma membrane: The membrane that surrounds the entire protoplast.

Plasmon: Genetic elements contained in the cytoplasm.

Plastids: Cell organelles involved in food synthesis; in storage of fats, starches, proteins, and various pigments; or in both.

Pleaching: A popular technique of training and pruning shrubs and trees into a wall. Very popular in Europe.

Pleasure ground: City parks may which has large reserve areas for playing games is called pleasure ground.

Pleiotropy: The phenomenon of a single major gene affecting more than one character.

Plinth: A plinth is a slab or block on which a column, pedestal, or statue sits. A plinth may also be the bottom portion of stones used to support a wall.

Plug system: A highly automated seedling production system in which seeds are direct seeded into individual cells in a plug tray by automatic seeders and covered by a germination mix, little seedlings are transplanted into flats or bedding plants pack and grown to size for sale.

Plugging: A method of lawn establishment involving the use of small pieces of sod.

Plumose: Feather like with long fine hairs which further have fine secondary hairs.

Plumule: Primary stem-bud of an embryo as it develops from the seed in germination.

Plunging: The insertion of planted –up container into a trench in winter and then covering with peat or sand.

Plur-annuals: These are perennials but flower in the first year and do not survive usefully another year.

Pocket garden: A small growing area planted with miniature and dwarf varieties.

Pod: Dry, one chambered fruit developing from a simple pistil and dehiscing by both the margins *e.g.*, pea, bean, *etc.*

Polar nuclei: Two centrally located nuclei in the embryo sac that unite with the second sperm cell in a triple fusion to develop endosperm.

Polarity: The state of having two opposite poles, *i.e.*, a top and a bottom.

Polianthes rose: Dwarf type rose with miniature flowers borne in cluster and having free flowering and perpetual bearing habit.

Pollarding: Lopping or removing the crown, which afterwards send out new shoots or branches.

Pollen compatibility: Ability of the pollen tube to grow through a style and reach the ovule in time to effect fertilization.

Pollen shedder: In hybrid seed production involving male sterility, the plants of male fertile line are termed as pollen shedders.

Pollenizer: Trees which are interplanted to pollenize the self unfruitful or partially fruitful varieties to set a good crop.

Pollination: The transfer of pollen from an anther to a stigma.

Pollinators: The agency by which pollen is transferred from an anther to a stigma.

Pollinium: Pollen mass consisting of all the pollen grains in an anther locule.

Polyadelphous stamens: When the filaments are united into a number of bundles.

Polyandry: The condition of one female having numerous male mates.

Polychromatic colour scheme: In this scheme every colours are used to create a riot of colour. Neighbouring plants need to be considered throughout the garden.

Polygamous: A species bearing both unisexual and bisexual flowers on the same or on different plants.

Polygenes: A series of multiple genes with small and cumulative effect which produce continuous variation in the phenotypes; quantitative characters are governed by these genes.

Polymerization: Chemical union of two or more molecules of the same kind to form a new compound having the same elements in the same proportions, but a higher molecular weight and different physical properties.

Polypetalous: A flower having separate petals and not joined as in Begonia, Candytuft.

Polyploid: An organism having more than two identical or distinct genomes, *e.g.*, triploid (3x), tetraploid (4x), *etc.*

Polyploidy: A condition in which a cell nucleus has more than two complete sets of chromosomes for the species.

Polysepalous: When the sepals in a calyx remain free from each other.

Pomander: It is derived from French word "pomme d'ambre" meaning an apple of amber, a ball made of perfume such as ambergris, musk or civet.

Pompon chrysanthemum: A group of chrysanthemum characterized by compact, tightly headed flowers ranging from little buttons to more than 5 cm in diameter without any visible centre, *e.g.*, Maharaja, Apsara, *etc.*

Pompon dahlia: Fully double and small globular flower heads, the florets are incurved at margin, short, blunt at the tip forming a honeycomb structure, *e.g.*, Duston stone, Gold drop, Tam Tam, *etc.*

Pompon: A Flower which is small and globular.

Porogamy: Penetration of the pollen tube through the micropyle.

Portico: Literally translated, a portico is a porch with the term being originated by followers of Palladio who first created this architectural style of design. Porticos consist of colonnades that are supported by pedimented roofs of varying heights and depths.

Pot clip: Some support is necessary to hold the plant until it becomes established in the pot. This could be facilitated by pot clip made by bending run of the pot and is held there with a small ring. It not only is a good support and stake for the plant, but also can be used for hanging the plants when necessary.

Pot-bound: The growing of roots over each other and around the bottom of the pot as a result of limited space.

Pot-mum: A modern method of pot plant production in which cuttings are planted directly in small sized pots.

Pot-porris: Pot-porris a special dried floral arrangement is the mixture of sweet smelling leaves, spices, seeds, roots and distilled essential oil which is filled in pillows or sachets.

Pre-cooling: It is the removal of field heat from cut flowers, in which temperature is brought down from 25-30°C to 1-2°C in less than hour time either through hydro-cooling or mechanical refrigeration.

Pre-curing: A treatment prior to soft wood grafting where the scion attached to mother plant is kept in a leafless condition for 7-10 days for better graft success.

Pre-disposition: Tendency of some non-genetic factors such as, abiotic stresses to effect susceptibility of plants to diseases.

Pre-germination: Germination of seeds usually until the radical just emerges before sowing.

Prepotency: The capacity of a parent to impress characters on its off-spring.

Preserving: Ornamental plant material is commonly preserved (plasticized) by treatment with humectants. Humectants are hygroscopic chemicals, which help to maintain the suppleness of dried plants material by attracting water vapour from the surrounding atmosphere. The preserved plant material is less brittle than the dried material, making it less prone to shattering and mechanical damage.

Pressing: A drying technique that preserves plant materials in a two dimensional form.

Prey crop: The crop which is grown with the purpose of eliminating any undesirable plant through physical or its allelopathic effect.

Pricking: A method raising secondary nursery for the crops having very small seeds and in the case of high density showing, it helps to develop a thinner stand in the nursery. The operation of transferring the young seedlings to another pan or tray.

Prickles: Defensive organs of plants irregularly distributed on the plant body which are usually curved, unbranched and commonly used for climbing.

Primary colours: The foundation colours of red, yellow, and blue which cannot be created by mixing any other colours.

Primary metabolites: Substances that (i) are found in essentially all plants and (ii) play reasonably well understood roles in the physiology of the plant *e.g.* carbohydrates and proteins.

Primed seed: Seed soaked in a specific solution to initiate physiological processes for quicker germination.

Primordial: Initials or beginning of plant organs.

Principles of design: The principles are the fundamental concepts of composition—proportion, order, repetition, and unity—that serve as guidelines to arrange or organize the features to create an aesthetically pleasing or beautiful landscape.

Production phase: A phase requiring 1-6 years which covers all aspects of the bulb production leading to the sale of forcing size of bulbs.

Programming phase: The temperature treatments being subjected to flowering bulbs from the time of harvesting until being placed under glass house conditions.

Prop roots: Roots that are produced from the main stem and often from branches and grown vertically or obliquely downwards and penetrate into the soil and act as pillars supporting the main stem and the branches or the plant as a whole as seen in *Ficus, Pandanus, etc.*

Propagation case: A transparent and enclosed container used for raising seedlings.

Propagule: Plant part which when separated will produce a new individual.

Prophyll: The bract like laves subtending the entire plant or inflorescence in monocots as in Gladiolus.

Proportion or scale: Proportion is concerned with the size relationship of the features of the landscape. It is the relation of one thing with the other in magnitude. The space allotted for different features should be in right proportion as under: Lawn (25-30 per cent), Paths (20 per cent), herbaceous borders (20 per cent), Shrubbery (15-20 per cent), Trees (15 per cent), Buildings (35-40 per cent). In the stairs the tred and riser should be right proportion for indoor and outdoor rooms. Other features should be right proportion.

Propping: The practice of providing support to a plant with the help of crossed bamboo poles to prevent it from falling off.

Prospect: It is the view of scenery, natural or manmade, through an opening such as window or a gap in the foliage of trees.

Prostrate: A condition of growth where plants grow flat on the ground.

Protandrous: In a flower where mature anthers release the pollen before stigma receptivity but when it continues even after the stigma receptivity it is known as incomplete protandry which enables self pollination.

Protandry: The condition in which pollen is shed before the stigma is receptive in the same flower as in *Annona* sp. (complete potandry) and the condition in which pollen shedding begins before the stigma is receptive but continues afterwards so that self-pollination can take place as in some *Passiflora* sp.

Proteranthous: A situation in plant growth where appearance of the leaves precedes the flowering.

Protocorm: A small bulb-like structure formed as an orchid seed begins to grow. Meristem embryoids form protocorms before growing leaves and roots.

Protogyny: The condition in which the pistils become receptive before the stamens shed their pollen.

Protoplasm: The living matter in the cells, referred to as the 'physical basis of life'.

Protoplast fusion: The techniques of in vitro union of two protoplasts into somatic hybrids.

Pruning: The removal of any undesirable part is termed as pruning. It encourages new healthy shoots to develop and keeps the plants in desired shape or form.

Pseudo bulb: Pseudo bulb is a specialized storage structure produced aerially, consisting of an enlarged fleshy section of the stem made up of one to several nodes and is very common in orchids *viz., Cattleya, Cymbidium, Laelia* and *Dendrobium.*

Pseudocompatibility: The phenomenon of a functional incompatibility system but self-seed is produced in amounts ranging from an occasional few to levels approaching true self-incompatibility.

Pseudodominance: Apparent expression of the recessive allele in a heterozygous individual when the dominant allele is absent.

Pteridophyta: The highest group of cryptogams in which the plant body is differentiated into rhizome or an erect stem, well-developed green leaves and true roots.

Public area: The part of the house that faces the street or public area is that area of the home garden which is viewable from the street or is seen by anyone coming to the home. This area conveys the initial impression about the residents of the house. Poorly designed and ill-kept landscape leads to sloppiness, sparsely planted or rigidly pruned leads to austerity and walled as a courtyard projects the sense of seclusion. The main functions of public area are: to blend the house with its surroundings. To provide a pleasant and readily accessible entry to the house.

Puffer: A completely rotted bulb due to *Penicillium* infection but with intact tunic or skin which on rupturing releases a large mass of spores.

Pulsing or loading: It consists of placing the lower portion of cut flower stems in solution containing high percentage of sugar and germicide for a period of few hours to two days. Specific formulations developed vary with the floral species as sucrose 2-20 per cent for 12-48 hours at 20-27°C and relative humidity 80-100 per cent under 2000-2500 lux cool light.

Pure line: Progeny a single homozygous, self pollinated plant.

Q

Quantitative long day plant: Plant that is not imbibed from flowering by short day treatments but hastened by long day treatments.

Quantitative trait: A trait that is controlled by a group of genes at different loci with each allelic pair having a specific quantitative effect on the expression of the trait.

Quick hedge: A hedge of living plants, particularly hawthorn. Also called QUICKSET.

Quiescent: Invisible growth *i.e.* state of rest.

Quilled chrysanthemum: A group of chrysanthemum in which the ray florets are tubular like a quill with lips which may be opened or closed.

Quilling of florets: Malformation of flowers of chrysanthemum resulting in the uneven of flatten appearance of flowers caused by low temperature during development or water stress during flower development.

Quoin: A quoin is a stone laid in a grouping to create angles and corners of a structure's wall usually in contrasting material for an artistic effect.

R

Race: An assemblage of organisms that exhibits similarities but is not sufficiently distinct from other forms to constitute a species.

Raceme: An indeterminate and unbranched inflorescence composed of pedicellate flowers or Inflorescence where the main axis is elongated and bears laterally a number of flowers which are all stalked, the lower flowers having longer stalks than the upper ones, as in *Caesalpinia, etc.*

Rachis: The flower-bearing portion of an inflorescence.

Radial landscape style: The shapes are created from an underlying radial grid versus a square grid. The garden simply radiates from central point following the concentric patterns and creates very interesting and dynamic spaces. It is also called circular style.

Radiation: Emission and propagation of energy through the medium of space or material. Radiations may be ionizing and non-ionizing. Ionizing radiations are of two types, electromagnetic (X-rays and Gamma rays) and particulate (Alfa, Beta, Protons and Neutrons) radiations. Non-ionizing radiation include UV rays.

Radicum: These plants are special in that their stems have roots that will cling as they grow vertically or grow over the ground. Ivy is a good example

Rainy season annuals: These annuals can withstand heavy rains and high humidity coupled with high temperature. These are sown during May-June.

Raking: The gentle use of a spring tine rake or similar tool to remove fallen leaves or surface debris from the lawn.

Rambler rose: Roses which have long pliable stems, bloom once a year and produce small flowers in large clusters, originated from a cross between *Rosa mutiflora* and *Rosa wichuraiana.* This type of rose is not suitable for the plains of India.

Rambler: It has neither any modified organ for climbing nor it coils around the support, but climb on its own.

Rampart: Ramparts consist of embankments that are usually topped with parapets that come together to create large, defensive fortifications.

Randomized block design: An experimental design where the number of blocks is equal to the number replication of each treatment and each block is divided into homogeneous plots of equal size, within which the treatment are applied randomly.

Ray florets: These florets surround the disc-florets and comparatively longer and varied in shape, color and direction of growth and contain only the female reproductive parts; characteristics of Asteraceae.

Reaction wood: Wood produced in response to a stem that has lost its vertical position.

Receding colours: Colours such as blue and violet which are not highly visible from a distance and seem to become smaller or disappear (recede) because of their colour.

Rectilinear landscape style: This approach ensures much more efficient use of space without wastage like in curvilinear or radial pattern. This style is also ideal for small spaces or restricted sites like city gardens enclosed by fences and walls with rectangular or regular shape.

Reeds: Tall grasses that grow in shallow water. The common reed, or ashi, *Phragmites communis*; the Japanese reed, *P. macer*; and the giant reed, *Arundo donax,* all have been dwarfed for bonsai.

Reefers: A trade term used to designate the controlled temperature containers for transporting bulbs.

Reflexed chrysanthemum: A group of chrysanthemum characterised by large sized flowers in which petals are curved outward and downward, *e.g.,* W.A. Reid, Kasturba Gandhi, *etc.*

Registered seed: It is the progeny of foundation seed that is so handled as to maintain satisfactory genetic identity and purity and that has been approved and certified by a certifying agency. This class of seed is used for the production of certified seed.

Relative humidity: The ratio of water vapour in a given quantity of air to the total weight of water vapour that quantity of air can hold at a given temperature expressed as a percentage.

Remontant: Repeatedly bearing flowers in the course of a single season.

Repetition: Repetition is created by the repeated use of elements or features to create patterns or a sequence in the landscape.

Repotting: The transfer of a plant from one pot to another and replacing the soil mixture with the fresh one. Periodical repotting should be carried out for perennials, as the overgrown roots system produces pressure against the sides of the pot and further growth of the root system will be affected, resulting in the arrest of the normal plant growth.

Resistance: The ability of an organism to exclude or overcome, partially or completely the effect of pathogen or other damaging factors.

Rest period: Physiological condition of the buds of many woody perennial species when they do not expand into flowers or leafy shoots even under suitable growing conditions and this rest influence is broken after exposure to sufficient cold.

Resupination: A process by which the lip of orchid flower, the uppermost petal, becomes the lower most one through a remarkable twisting of the pedicellate ovary.

Retaining Walls: Retaining walls are structures built to support soil or water and prevent either from advancing forward.

Retarded Bulbs: A term used for retarding the bulbs to produce delayed flowering *e.g.* Dutch iris bulbs after harvesting are stored dry at 30 °C.

Retardent: A growth regulator which slows down or reduces growth such as elongation or leaf expansion. Growth does not cease.

Rhizocaline: A substance present in the cotyledons, leaves and buds which stimulate the rooting in cuttings. It is a complex of orthodihydroxy phenol, auxin and an enzyme probably of polyphenol oxidase type.

Rhizome: Rhizome is a specialized underground stem structure in which the main stem axis grows horizontally at or just below the ground surface. The important examples are *Alstroemeria, Bamboo, Canna, Convallaris, Hydechium, Iris* and *Zantedeschia.*

Rhizosphere: Portion of the soil in the immediate vicinity of plant roots in which the abundance and composition of the microbial population are influenced by the presence of roots.

Rhythm: Rhythm is an easy connected path along which the eye will travel in any direction from one point to another without disturbance. The important examples of rhythm are: The action of a dancer in case of Punjabi folk dance in which the eye travels from one dancer to another without disturbance. When a stone is thrown in a water tank, the waves are seen in the rhythmic action. The beat of marshal music.

Ribbing: A series of narrow lines of long and short grass, at right angles to the direction of mowing.

Rikka: Large arrangements used in large recesses and temples. Literally "Standing Flowers".

Ring budding: A method of budding in which a ring of bark is removed from the stock and a similar one containing a healthy bud is removed from the bud stick and then slipped over the rootstock, practiced in ber.

Rock garden: (1) A garden constructed of rock outcropping in a manner to appear as a naturalized design or wild flowers. (2) One of the most attractive and interesting feature of bigger gardens where small builders or rocks and soil are arranged in such a fashion that conditions are created for the growth of different, plants such as annuals, succulents, bog plants and ferns.

Rock plant: A small plant (eg an alpine) that grows among rocks or is otherwise particularly suited to growing in a rock garden.

Rock wool: A human made growing media component made from an igneous rock, basalt. It consists of fibers similar in an appearance to cotton candy. Rock wool is used extensively in hydroponic operations. Rock wool has good water holding capacity and good aeration. It is slightly alkaline and has a low cation exchange capacity.

Rockery: The garden developed on the rock with particular rock or other ornamental plants.

Rodenticides Substances that prevent, inhibit, destroy, kill rodents (Class *Mammalia, Order Rodentia*).

Rolling: To make the soil compact in lawn; rolling is required.

Roof Garden: A garden created on a flat roof, often above a block of flats or a departmental store, to which all materials and supplies have to be elevated.

Root pruning: Removal of portions or all of the younger roots with a view to develop extensively branched root systems at the base of the plant, practiced in rose.

Rooting media: Materials such as sand, peat, perlite, vermiculite or soil into which the basal ends of the cuttings are placed for root development.

Rootstock: The bottom part of a graft that is in contact with the soil and not allowed to produce side shoots.

Rosaceous: (1) Arranged like the five petals of a normal rose. (2) Belonging to the order of which Rosa is a genus.

Rosary: A rose garden, or a rose bed in a mixed garden; a favourite expression in Victorian times but seldom heard today.

Rosebud: As in tuberous begonias where flowering buds are slightly conical with tepals gradually infolding and where the centre is properly defined.

Rostellum: The male and female part of orchid being separated by a flap or projection of a tissue called rostellum. *e.g. vanilla.*

Round bulbs: In Dutch Iris and Narcissus it is shape of the bulb produced by a non flowering plant.

Rugose: Rough and wrinkled

Rushes and sedges: The common scouring-rush, *Equisetum hyemale*, and the umbrella plant, *Cyperus alternifolius* var, gracilis, make very elegant dwarf potted plants (bonsai) for indoor decoration.

S

Saba-miki bonsai: Also called Split Trunk Bonsai which suggests an ancient tree with decayed trunk and torn branches.

Saddle grafting: Method of grafting in which the top of the stock is cut first transversely, and then two upward cuts are given on either side to form a wedge, and a cleft is made in the scion so that it fits tightly over the stock; joint then sealed. Used more in herbaceous than on woody plants.

Sakai: A Japanese art of growing and dwarfing plants in pots which is ideal for space-starved situations. It is miniature replicas of a natural landscape. Sakai means living landscape and is also known as Table Top Landscaping.

Sanctuary: An area constituted by the competent authority in which killing and capturing of any form of wild life is prohibited and the boundaries and character of which are sacrosanct.

Sapling: A young tree characterized by the absence of dead bark with vigorous height growth.

Saprophyte: Organism which obtains organic matter in solution from dead and decaying tissues of plants or animals.

Saprophytic orchids: Orchids that are devoid of chlorophyll grow on decayed organic matter and absorb food materials from the host.

Scaffold Branch: The main branch growing from the trunk of a tree.

Scalding: A physiological disorder of green house plants occurring due to rapid fluctuations in the temperature, draughts, hot dry atmosphere and fumes. This causes browning and withering of leaf edges and brown or whitish spots on leaves, browning and withering of young shoots.

Scale: The landscape design principle that creates proportionately among design elements.

Scaling: Technique used to propagate foundation stock, wherein the scales of bulbs are removed and planted. This produces numerous scale bulblets from a single mother scale.

Scalping: Scalping is all too familiar high spots shaved bare by the mower. A cylinder mower is more likely to cause scalping than a rotary model.

Scandent: Plants with climbing stem.

Scape bending: A phenomenon in cut gerbera which is caused by excessive bacterial growth in vase solution that results in bending of the portion just below the bud

Scape: An unbranched inflorescence with one flower.

Scarification: Abrasion or chemical treatment of seed coat in order to speed up water intake and induce germination.

Scarifying: The vigorous use of a rake or rake like tool to remove thatch; this job is done in autumn – never in spring.

Scenic Easement: Scenic easement is the legal means of keeping a site's beautiful views and vistas aesthetically protected from changes to existing features without the approval of the government.

Scion root: Root which originates from the variety grafted or budded on to a rootstock as distinct from a root originating from the rootstock.

Scion: The plant part that is the top part of a graft and grows to become the desired shoot.

Sciophyte: Plant which is shade loving.

Sclerophyte: A plant adapted to a climate of wet winter and hot dry summer characterized by thick hard, usually small, evergreen leaves capable of functioning during winter and withstanding the dry summer.

Sclerotization: Hardening and darkening of the cuticle. The hardening is owing to the deposition of sclerotizing-substances in the exocuticle.

Scooping: A method of propagation in certain bulbs such as Hyacinthus, in which apical dominance is terminated by scooping out the basal plate of the bulb to encourage more bulblet formation.

Scoring: Similar to scooping, however, the basal plate is not removed. Two cuts that cross the basal plate are made about a ¼ inch deep.

Scrambling plant: A fast-growing climber with long stems and often thorns that entangle with other plants growing close by, *e.g.* climbing roses, brambles and Russian vine.

Scree garden: It means growing of high altitude alpines in the sloping beds formed by accumulation of weathered rock debris forming a heap at the base of cliff, hill or mountain slope but no water is supplied beneath the surface.

Screen: A vegetative or constructed hedge or fence used to block wind, undesirable views, noise, glare and the like, as part of in landscape design; also known as 'screen planting' and 'buffer plantation'.

Scrub: Vegetation consisting of stunted trees, bushes and other plants growing in an arid area.

Season flowers: Extremely succulent plants which come into flowering in a particular season(s) in a year.

Secondary colours: Colours creating by mixing the adjacent, primary colours, orange, green and violet.

Secretion: The movement, either by diffusion or active transport, of materials out of a plant or in to a space where it can accumulate for storage.

Sectorial chimera: A chimera where genetically different tissues are situated side by side in the same plant part.

Secund: Where all the parts of the leaves or flowers are born along one side of the axis or appear so due to twisting of the stalk.

Sedges/rushes: Sedges have stems that are triangular in shape and solid, while rush stems are round. Both sedges and rushes favour a moist habitat.

Sediment: The product of erosion processes; the solid material, both mineral and organic, that is in suspension, is being transported or has been moved from its site of origin by air, water, gravity or ice.

Seed ball: It is the so called seed of beet and palak which is actually the aggregation of two or more fruits that are held together by swollen perianth base thus forming an irregular cork like body.

Seed bed: A prepared area in which seed are sown.

Seed certification: A legally sanctioned scientific system for quality control of seed multiplication and production which consists of the following control measures: administrative check on the origin of propagating material, field inspection, sample inspection, bulk inspection and control plot testing.

Seed garden: A plantation usually of a superior race raised or treated for the production of seed.

Seed Germination: A sequence of events in a viable seed starting with water imbibition and leading to embryo growth and development.

Seed Longevity: A measure of how long seed remains viable.

Seed pallet: A coherent seed ball made up of one or more seeds compressed in various materials like clay, fertilizer, rodent and insect repellents *etc.*

Seed testing: A series of tests on purity, moisture content and germination of seed sample to determine its quality.

Seed viability: The promotion of seed in a lot that is capable of germinating.

Seed: A matured ovule that consists of an embryo, its stored food and protective coverings; it also commonly includes the ovules of one seeded dry indehiscent fruits like paddy, wheat, *etc.*

Seedling: The juvenile stage of a plant grown from seed.

Seismonasty: Movement of plant part brought about by mechanical stimuli such as contact with a foreign body, poking with any hard object, drops of rain, a gust of wind, *etc., e.g. Mimosa, Averrhoa, etc.*

Selection: Different reproduction rates of different genotypes which change the frequency of alleles and genotypes in a population. It aims at isolating the desirable one(s) from the mixture of numerous genotypes in the population; most important step in plant breeding.

Selective herbicide: A weed killer formulated to be effective only against particular plants, such as annual grasses or broadleaved species.

Self pollinated annuals: Lupine, sweet pea, salvia, saponaria, carnation, sweet william, double aster, clianthus and gypsophila.

Self seed: The natural propagation of a plant by the germination of its seeds around it.

Semi double chrysanthemum: A group of chrysanthemum in which the ray florets are strap like in more than five whorls with conspicuous disc.

Semi hardwood cuttings: Cuttings made from woody, broad-leaved ever-green species such as ligustrum and holly.

Semi trap flower: Flowers into which pollinators get in through a conspicuous opening, but the interior of flower is so constructed that they are to leave by a certain route, and during which they pick up or have pollen thrown on them.

Semi-evergreen: (of a tree or shrub) retaining most of its leaves during a mild winter, although tending to shed them in severe weather.

Semi-hard wood: An alternative term for semi-ripe wood.

Seminal propagation: The increase of plants by sexual processes, *e.g.* through seeds and spores contained within the original plant.

Seminal: Potentially capable of development; related to seed or germ.

Sen Rin Tsukuri: In this style, the plant is designed to a geometrical shape (6-10 concentric circles in steeped manner) and it is trained in such a way that about 200-300 blooms are formed per plant having an approximate height of 153-183 cm and a diameter of 183-244 cm.

Senescence: Senescence is the final phase in ontology of the organ in which a series of normally irreversible events initiated that leads to cellular breakdown and death of the organ.

Sepaline tube: In some orchids like *Physosiphon,* the sepals are united together and form a tube like structure known as sepaline tube.

Sepaloid: Resembling a sepal.

Sepals: The leaf like structures encasing a flower bud and later subtending the open flower.

Separation: A method of propagation in which underground structures of plants are divided not by cutting but by breaking along natural lines between segments.

Serpentine layering: Layering done by alternately covering and exposing the long slender shoots of the plant over their entire length in the ground. Slanting cuts are given at the points where the shoots are to be layered, practiced in *Jasminum, Clematas, etc.*

Service area: The part of the house that is hidden from public view and where utility accessories and unflattering items are stored.

Shade garden: Shade gardening refers to growing of shade loving plants under shady conditions. The shady conditions may be natural tree shades or artificial shade created using protected structures such as conservatories, shade net houses, *etc.*

Shade plant: Plants which require low light intensity for growth. *e.g., Nolina recurvata, Peperomia, etc.*

Shade trees: Fast growing trees which provide shade to other crops like coffe, tea, cocoa for their growth and development in tropics, *e.g., Erythrina, Grevillea, etc.*

Shakan bonsai: A slanting trunk bonsai which imitates a tree growing at right angles to a mountain slope. Its foliage is generally thicker on the side facing the sun. Sometimes this style is called Han-Kengai Bonsai or Semi-Cascade Bonsai.

Shattering: Abscission of snapdragon florets caused by ethylene or pollination.

Sheath: The tubular portion of the leaf, which wraps around or encloses the stem. Sheaths can be described as cylindrical, flattened, or compressed.

Sheath-life: It refers to the span up to which the perishable commodities can be kept at consumable and marketable stage after harvest.

Shelterbelt: A belt of trees and/or shrubs maintained for the purpose of shelter from wind, sun, snow-drift, *etc.* Syn. Protective-belt. Shelter-belts are generally more extensive than windbreaks covering areas larger than single farm and sometimes whole regions on a planned pattern. Syn. Wind break; Snow break.

Shito bonsai. Tiny bonsai plants in 2.5 cm pots that can actually be held on the tip of a finger. Also called Finger-tip bonsai.

Sho-chiku-bai: Enduring happiness. This is expressed in an arrangement made with a combination of pine, bamboo and plum blossoms and is created for all important occasions and for New Year.

Sho-kengai bonsai: See Kengai Bonsai.

Short day plants: Plant that flower when the day length is shorter than the critical.

Show dahlia: A group of dahlia in which flower heads are fully double, almost globular with smaller central florets and margin of the florets are incurved, tubular and cap-shape *e.g.* Model, standard, *etc.*

Shrub: A shrub is a woody or semi-woody perennial plant with the little or no trunk and grows up to a height from 50 cm to less than four meters or It may be defined as a perennial plant having many woody branches arising from the base of the plant. The plant whose basal portion is woody and upper shoots are soft is called sub-shrub.

Shrubbery border: Area of the garden devoted exclusively for growing shrubs planted in a row or rectangular fashion is known as shrubbery border.

Shrubbery: An area of ground in which a collection of shrubs is planted.

Shy bearing habit: It marks the habit of flowering and fruiting regularly but to a very little extent.

Sib mating: Mating among individuals related by direct pedigree, such as brother-sister mating.

Sib: Progeny of same parents derived from different gametes.

Silica Gel: A type of drying agent available as white crystals or colours-indicator crystals that change colours when the desiccant is too moist to effectively use.

Simplicity: A landscape design principle that employs a number of strategies to reduce excessive variation and distractions in the landscape. The landscape designer must develop simplicity in the design, to provide a restful setting for the outdoor living in the property area. Simplicity in design is achieved through several ways: Repetition of same species for similar form (silhouette), habit or color and construction material, Smooth flowing of silhouette or grouping of plants, avoid too many species in a small area.

Single cross: The first generation hybrid between two specified inbred lines.

Single dahlia: Flower heads not exceeding 10 cm diameter and having one row of ray floret surrounding the central disc florets, suitable for bedding purpose *e.g.* kokette, Frances, *etc.*

Site analysis: An inventory of existing natural and manmade features at a proposed landscape site or site analysis is the second stage of planning in which an inventory of the existing property items including the architecture of the house, landscape, view points, soil, climate, plot size, *etc.* are prepared. Both good and bad points are mentioned for developing a successful home landscape.

Site Plan: A drawing of the locations of plants and inanimate objects in a landscape.

Skeletonizing: As the name implies, this treatment eliminates all tissues but the "skeleton" or veins of leaves. Skeletonized leaves lend an interesting, lacy appearance to dried arrangements. Heavy-textured leaves are the best choices for this method of preservation.

Skyline: Garden meets the sky in its vertical dimension. This principle is referred to as skyline.

Slab side: A disorder in carnation which refers to uneven opening of flower buds resulting in the petals protruding on one side only, giving an asymmetrical and lopsided shape to the flower.

Sleepiness: A disorder causing temporary or permanent wilting of carnation or lily flowers by exposure to ethylene. It is due to exposure to ethylene or water stress or higher temperature which can be controlled by spraying of STS 0.4mM before harvesting or as a replacement for STS, cut flowers can be kept in 1-MCP (Methyl Cyclo-Propene) 10-20 ppb for 6-12 hours.

Sleeve fence: Fence resembling the shape of a long sleeve of a lady's kimono which is made in the Japanese garden for the purpose of screening.

Slope: The gradient of the surface of the ground, expressed as the angle which the surface makes with the horizontal surface.

Sod: A shallow (1-3 inches) of topsoil that is bound by grass roots and usually harvested and sold in narrow strips.

Soe: This is the second tallest line representing "Man". It is symbolized in the Sogetsu diagrams by a square.

Soft landscaping: The natural elements in landscape design, such as plant materials and the soil itself.

Softwood: Wood produced by a conifer.

Sogetsu: Meaning "Grass Moon." The name of Japanese school of Ikebana.

Soil conditioners: Chemicals which are added to maintain physical condition of the soil, *e.g.*, cellulose gums, lignin derivatives, silicates, *etc.*

Soil erosion: The wearing away of the land surface by geological agents such as water, wind and ice.

Soil profile: A vertical cross-section of the soil showing the various layers or horizons that have developed over the period of soil formation.

Soil structure: The arrangement of primary soil particles in to secondary particles, units or peds.

Soil texture: The relative percentage of sand, silt and clay in a soil.

Soil: The solid portion of the earth's crust consisting of mineral, air, water and organic matter in which plants grow.

Soilless culture: The collectivity of methods used to grow plants in media that do not consist of mineral soil.

Solarization: The light dependent absorption of O_2 and the release of CO_2 that causes bleaching of chloroplast which is evident when plants are moved from shade to sunny condition.

Solitary flowers: Flowers those borne singly.

Somaclonal variation: Heritable variation that arises spontaneously as callus forms on a tissue culture medium.

Somatic hybridization: Production of hybrid cells by fusion of two protoplasts with different genetic makeup.

Spadix: A spike of flowers on a thick and fleshy axis often subtended by spathe as in Araceae.

Spathe: A modified often papery bract or leaf enclosing the inflorescence as in Araceae. The attractive colourful plant that is traded is actually a modification of the leaf which is botanically called 'spathe' as in Anthurium.

Spatial arrangement: The pattern of distribution of plants over the ground which determines the shape of the area available to the individual plant.

Spatulate: Shape like a spatula, *i.e.* broad and somewhat rounded at the top and narrower at the base.

Speaking flowers: Speaking flowers are those in which the flower petals are embossed with images, photos or short messages without harming and shortening the life of flowers.

Spear: The shoot which is the edible part of the asparagus.

Species: A category of taxonomic classification lower than a genus or subgenus and above that of a subspecies or variety.

Specimen plant: A plant with attractive features that is used to fulfil the principle of focalization or emphasis in an arrangement.

Spectabilis: Remarkable, conspicuous.

Spider chrysanthemum: A group of chrysanthemum where the rayflorets are tubular and elongated but slightly curved with coiled or hooked tips.

Spike flower: Flower stems having a series of short-stemmed flowers progressing in maturity from the tip.

Spike: The inflorescence in which the main axis is elongated and the lower flowers open earlier than the upper ones as in raceme, but the flowers are sessile, seen in tuberose, amaranthus, *etc.*

Spiking: After three or four years of constant use, turf becomes compact. The root system is restricted and the grass dries out due to old grass stems and roots that prevent watering, aeration and nutrients reaching the soil. For this turf should be spiked by inserting fork about 10cm deep at 10 -15 cm interval.

Spilt complementary: A colour scheme which combines one hue with the two hucs that is on each side of its direct complement.

Spines: Modifications of leaves which serve the purpose of defence mechanism, water conservation, *etc.*

Spitting: The abscission or release of the entire floral stalk or inflorescence from the basal plate during forcing in Hyacinthus.

Split complementary harmony: Combination of primary or an intermediate colour with the colour on either side of its complement form split complementary harmony. *e.g.* yellow with red purple and blue purple, yellow orange with blue and purple.

Splitting of nodes in carnations: Poor shoots developed through gaps, poor flower quality, boron deficiency, apply boron @ 2g/m^2.

Splitting of the calyx: The biggest problem with harvested carnations. This condition, when the calyx splits, petals spill out and the flowers appears miss happen, is caused by fluctuations of temperatures and is more common with some cultivars and than others.

Spontaneous mutation: Mutation that occur in natural populations without any mutagenic treatment.

Spoon chrysanthemum: A group of chrysanthemum where the ray florets are tubular up to some length from the base and then open like a spatula.

Sport: A mutant that is inherited and transmitted to progeny.

Spot elevation: In surveying and contour layout, an existing or proposed elevation noted as a dot on the plan.

Spreader board: A flat piece of board with v-cuts at both ends that is forced between the stem and a branch with a narrow crutch to widen it.

Sprig: A piece of grass shoots. It may be a piece of stolon or rhizome or lateral shoot. Sprigging is a vegetative method of establishing a lawn.

Sprigging: Propagation of turf grasses by rhizomes or stolons placed in shallow furrows or small holes.

Spudding: Removal of weeds by cutting off below the soil surface.

Spur: A hollow, sac-like or tubular extension of the base of the lip, usually bearing nectar.

Staggered plant: Planting/sowing of a crop spread over an optimum period of planting to minimize risks, use labour/machinery more effectively, minimize competition (in intercropping) and to prolong the period of product supply to the market.

Staking: It is an act of fixing sticks sharpened at one-end into the soil near to the plants to provide support so that they may not bend or fall down.

Stalk: The petiole, peduncle, filament, stipe (stalk of the pistil) *etc.* which provide stem like support to their respective organs.

Stamen: The male part of flower consisting of anther and filament.

Stamenless sterility: A type of male sterility where stamens of a bisexual flower become rudimentary which is governed by single recessive gene.

Stamina sterility: A type of male sterility where only pistillate flowers are produced in some monoecious cucurbits which act as super female plant *e.g.*, gynoecious cucumber line.

Staminal carpellody: The transformation of stamens into fleshy carpel like structure during the early development of a flower.

Staminate: A male flower bearing stamens and no functional pistils.

Staminode: A structure appearing in the place of a stamen but bearing no pollen.

Star dahlia: A group of dahlia in which flower head is small, having 2-3 rows of pointed petals which overlap very slightly, forming a cup shaped appearance with a group of central disc florets *e.g.*, White star.

Stenting: A method was developed for quick propagation of roses under conditions prevailing in The Netherlands, based on cutting and grafting in one action and called "stenting" (to stent), being a contraction of the dutch words "stekken" (to strike a cutting) and "enten" (to graft). A piece of stem of the cultivar with one leaf and a dormant bud is grafted on a single internode of the rootstock. Formation of the graft union and of adventitious roots occurs simultaneously, resulting in a complete plant in 3 weeks. Absence of buds on the rootstock is essential to diminish wild suckering.

Stigma: The sticky upper surface of pistil which receives pollens.

Stionic influence: Reciprocal influence of stock and scion which determine the graft compatibility.

Stipe: The stalk-like support of a pistil, or other small organ such as pollinium.

Stock plant: Specially bred plant cultivar that serves as the source of material used in vegetative propagation.

Stolon: A stem that grows above ground and produces roots and new shoots at the nodes. Turfgrasses that have stolons are referred to as having a stoloniferous growth habit.

Stragglers or Ramblers: Some plants which fail in their attempt to climb but somehow manage to support themselves over the trunks, stems or branches of other plants are termed ramblers or stragglers.

Stratification: A method of breaking seed dormancy in which the imbibed seeds are subjected to a period of chilling to after-ripen the embryo.

Straw Nails: It is form of flower abortion in hyacinths where uppermost florets dry up.

Street/Outdoor Furniture: Items of furnishing in outdoor landscape.

Strewing: The scattering of flowers and loose petals on the ground.

Stump: The base of a tree or roots left in ground after falling.

Style: Part of the pistil between the stigma and the ovary in a flower through which the pollen tube grows.

Sub tropical climate: A climate hot in summer with a cool winter.

Suberin: A hydrophobic material that occurs on the inner surface of a cell wall.

Sub-shrub: The plant whose basal portion is woody and the upper shoots are soft *e.g., Impatiens balsamina, Catharanthus rosea, etc.*

Subterranean orchids: Underground orchids, - found in Australia *e.g. Rhizanthetta* and *Cryptanthemis.*

Succulent: A group of plants which stores water by means of swollen or fleshy stems, leaves or tuberous roots, *e.g.,* Agave, Sedum, *etc.*

Suckers: A shoot developing from an underground stem or the plants root.

Suiban: A flat container.

Summer season annuals: These annuals grow luxuriantly and produce flowers under high temperature. In north Indian plains these are sown in February-March, whereas in hills in March-April. Cosmos, gaillardia, gomphrena, kochia, marigold(few cultivators), portulaca, sunflower, tithonia, zinnia.

Sunken garden: It is laid below the ground level. Sunken garden arose the curiosity of the visitor is to move places to find out surprise store for him.

Support crop: Certain fast growing crops which act as a support to vine crops, *e.g., Erythrina indica.*

Surprise: One component should be hidden from the other either by gentle turn of road, or screening through shrubbery or pergolas. This principle is referred to as surprise.

Swale: A linear wide and shallow depression used to temporarily store, route or filter runoff. A swale may be grassed or lined.

Swamp: A completely or partially vegetated area subject to permanent inundation in stagnant or slowly flowing water.

Sward: Syn. Turf

Sweetening: It denotes the special odour being emitted by lily bulbs stored under anaerobic conditions.

Sword sucker: The sucker of banana which have well-developed base with narrow sword-shaped leaf blades at the early stage.

Symbiosis: An intimate physiological association of two or more species resulting in mutual benefit, *e.g.*, Rhizobium bacteria on the roots of legumes.

Symmetrical balance: Symmetrical balance is achieved when the same objects (mirror images) are placed on either side of an axis.

Sympathy Flowers: Flowers that are sent to a funeral home or funeral service to honour the deceased and to comfort the bereaved.

Sympetalous: The flowers having joined petals as in lilium.

Sympodial orchids: The orchids that are able to make separate new growths through the extension of rhizome and each new growth produce its own set of roots and sometimes possess pseudo bulb. The important examples are *Bulbophyllum, Cattleya, Cymbidium, Dendrobium, Gramatophyllum, etc.*

Synanthous: Where leaves appear with the flowers.

Synapsis: The pairing of homologous chromosomes at meiotic prophase.

Syncarpous: In a compound pistil when the carpels are united together into one ovary, as in dianthus.

Syndrome: A group of symptoms that occur together and represent a particular disease.

Synsepalum: Organ resulting from the fusion of the two longer sepals of a lady slipper orchid. It is found below and behind the lip or pouch.

Synthetic variety: First generation progenies derived by intercrossing a specific set of lines of cross pollinated crop having good general combining ability. So synthetic variety usually contain mixtures of seed that result from cross, self and sib fertilization. Inbred lines, clones, mass selected varieties and lines developed by recurrent selection or reciprocal recurrent selection are generally synthesized by intercrossing after testing their general combining ability to develop a synthetic variety.

Synthetic: Populations derived from *inter se* crossing (Interbreeding) in diallel fashion of a number of inbreds of known high *per se* performance and combining ability, and subsequently maintained by open pollination.

T

Tangible: A quality denoting something that can be physically touched.

Tap root: Root that is developed from the radical directly giving rise to the main root of the plant.

Taxonomy: The science of identifying, naming and classifying plants.

T-budding: Method of budding done by making a cut in the bark of the stock in the form of a "T" and inserting the bud under the bark, practiced in rose.

Tea rose: Profuse blooming rose with fragrance similar to the aroma of tea leaves.

Tender annuals: These annuals are grown under protected conditions from the vagaries of adverse weather conditions. Oxalis, pansy.

Tendril: Slender, filiform, spiral or hooked organ arising from stem or foliage, affording plants a means of obtaining support by climbing trees or other bodies.

Tepal: One of the segments of a flower in which sepals and petals are not differentiated.

Terrace garden: It is a garden arranged in various levels or terraces. Terrace gardening involves land raising and construction of steps, ramps, walls and paved paths as well as planting of lawn grasses and other plants. It is desirable to have plants on the terrace but it should be restricted to the edges so that the middle is left open for circulation.

Terrace: A raised, more or less levelled or horizontal strip of earth usually constructed on or nearly on a contour and designed to make the land suitable for tillage and to prevent accelerated erosion.

Terracing: Terracing is the process of creating walls for the purpose of holding soil in place on sloped landscaping.

Terrarium: Terrarium is the sophisticated technique of growing plants indoor inside transparent glass containers in a manner to make it a complete ecosystem. Nathaniel B. Ward grew ferns, mosses and palms in a covered container about 125 years back in London, U.K.

Terrestrial orchids: The orchids that are grown on the land with their fleshy roots in the soil, and require uniform supply of water and nutrients like ordinary plant, *e.g., Paphipedilum, Phaius, Calanthe, Cymbidium, Habenaia, Spathoglottis, Thunia etc.*

Tertiary colours: A mixture of primary and secondary colours. *e.g.* Blue-green, blue-violet, red-violet, red-orange, yellow-orange, and yellow-green. *Syn.* Intermediate colour

Testcross: The mating between an individual of unknown genotype for a certain trait and an individual that is homozygous recessive for the same trait.

Tetrazolium (TZ) test: A biochemical method for determining the viability of both dormant and non-dormant seeds by the appearance of red color when the seeds are soaked in 2, 3, 5-triphenyltetrazolium chloride solution.

Texture: Representation of the structure of any surface is known as texture.

Thalamus: The suppressed swollen end of the flower axis (Pedicel) on which the floral leaves *viz.* sepals, petals, stamens and carpels are inserted.

Thallophyta: Lower Cryptogams in which plant body is a thallus, *i.e.*, not differentiated into stem and leaf. It includes algae and fungi, *etc.*

Thatch: Accumulated undecomposed organic material between the turf and soil surface.

Thermo-negative class of chrysanthemum: Bud initiation occurs at low to high temperature (10-27°C) but high temperature delays development of buds.

Thermo-positive class of chrysanthemum: Low temperature between 10-27°C inhibit or delay bud initiation which occur more consistently at 16°C. High temperature over 27°C accelerates bud initiation but delay flowering.

Thermo-zero class of chrysanthemum: Flowering occurs at any temperature between 10-27°C, more consistently at 17°C night temperature.

Thicket: Any area that has a lot of miscellaneous undergrowth, generally of small shrubs, bushes, and vines.

Thinning out: Pruning off entire stems or branches to give remaining stems or branches more space and more reserve food.

Thinning: Removal of excessive vegetative growth to open the plant canopy and reduce the number of flowering branches for larger flowers.

Threshold character: Characters whose development depend on a specific environment.

Threshold: The concentration, level or intensity below which a physical or chemical agent does not produce its effect.

Thug: Thugs are invasive plants which takes over a garden. They are growing in the right conditions, but ironically thugs can make a statement when they are perennials in the right garden.

Tillage: Working the soil to destroy weeds or otherwise improve its characteristics.

Tiller: A lateral shoot, usually erect, that develops intravaginally from axillary buds. Turf grasses that spread by tillers (lack rhizomes or stolons) are referred to as having a bunch-type growth habit.

Tinting in carnations: A concentrated liquid or powder colour is mixed in small amount of warm pure water (37°C) and stems are placed in it. The color develops in different patterns on the petals after 10-24 hours.

Tinting: It is a useful value addition technique in flower crops where colour pigments are absent or light and dull. It is done by using edible dyes and stains such as food colours, feulgen stain, bromocresol blue, bromocresol green, phenol red, *etc.*

Tip layering: A type of layering in which the growing tips of trailing type shoots are bent down and buried in the soil to depth of 5-7.5 cm to form roots.

Tissue: A set of cells that function together.

Tokonoma: This is raised dais in the Japanese reception rooms on which flowers are arranged.

Toko-zukuri bonsai: A bonsai like the octopus style which resembles the waving tentacles of an octopus, a mode of bonsai still much appreciated in china.

Tomentose: A downy covering of tiny woolly and stiff hairs on leaves and other plant parts.

Tone: A chromatic change of pure hue by addition of black and white *ie.,* Grey.

Top dressing: Applying fertilizer to the surface of the soil while the plants are growing.

Top grafting: A method of grafting in which the cultivar of a tree is changed by grafting the main scaffold branches or the stem using a new cultivar.

Top pruning: Removal of branches or parts of branches in order to develop the proper framework or form of the tree.

Top working: A grafting procedure employed primarily to change the cultivar of the established plant either by grafting or by budding.

Topiary: It is the art of training and pruning of plants into formal shapes sometimes geometric or abstract but highly stylized.

Topping: Removal of the terminal bud with or without some of the small top leaves just before or after the emergence of a flower bud.

Topple in gladiolus: Breaking of spikes as florets open in the vase which is closely correlated with calcium content of stalk tissues.

Topple: A physiological disorder in gladiolus characterised by breaking of spikes after opening of the florets in the vase

Toppling of tulips: A physiological disorder characterised by the collapse of a small portion of the inter-node of the floral stalk just underneath the flower.

Topsoil: The uppermost layer of the soil.

Torus: A receptacle of a flower, the region in which floral parts are inserted. An elongated torus is a gynophore, the stalk of a pistil which raises it above the pistil.

Toss bouquet: A small wired and taped bouquet that is thrown by the bride to unmarried friends during a traditional part of the wedding reception activities.

Totipotency: The ability of a somatic cell to reproduce the entire plant somatically.

Traffic island: An open space at the cross-section of multichannel road protected with low fence and beautified with ornamental plants, statue, fountain, *etc.*

Trailers: It is similar to creepers.

Training: A process, by which a plant is tied, pruned, fastened or staked to give a proper shape.

Trait: A synonym of character with respect to function and performance, but less so with respect to form.

Transgenic: A cell or organism that contains a gene or genes inserted into them from other organisms.

Transgressive breeding: Isolation of recombinants possessing new characters or new intensity of traits surpassing both the parents in F_2 onwards, that is breeding through assembling the productivity alleles.

Transpiration: The loss of water from plant surfaces by evaporation and diffusion.

Transplant: A seedling or rooted cutting after it has been moved one or more times in a nursery, in contrast to a seedling planted out directly from the seed bed.

Transplanting shock: A temporary setback in growth suffered by fresh transplants due to adverse conditions.

Transplanting: Moving a plant from its place of origin to another location. Transplanting is the process of bodily lifting of mature and large plants from their position to a new position.

Trap flower: Similar to semitrap flower except that emergence of the pollinator is delayed until flower changes configuration.

Treatment: A particular set of experimental condition which is imposed on an experimental unit within the confines of a chosen design.

Tree: A woody plant, generally taller than 2.00 m, with a well-distinguished trunk or trunks

Tree grate: A metal grille, installed at the base of a tree otherwise surrounded by pavement that allows the free passage of air, water, and nutrients to the tree root, but does not interfere with the foot traffic.

Tree surgery: A pruning art involving removal of large limbs, cleaning and treating wounds, and bracing weak trunk and crotches.

Tree: Tree is a perennial plant having distinct trunk and crown at the top.

Trellis: A frame or lattice of wooden or iron bars crossing either at right angles or diagonally which is used to support climbing plants.

Trellising: Wire mesh, plastic nets, string or bamboo canes are used to support plants. Wire mesh or plastic nets having inner size of 10-15 cm squares are placed on the ground in three layers, which are erected at 20, 35 and 50 cm above the ground level with the growing plants. String or rope is erected in three rows at same distance along the rows.

Trench layering: Method of layering which consists of placing a stem in a shallow trench and cover with soil and after producing roots from the nods, the new individual is removed from the mother plant, also called continuous layering.

Triad: A colour scheme combining three equally spaced hues on the colour wheel, such as the primary colours or the secondary colours.

Triadic: It is the use of three colours in the triangle Yellow, Red and Blue, or Violet, Orange and Green.

Triallel: Three way hybrids of a particular set of males and females.

Triangular system: A system of planting in which trees are planted as in the square system but the plants in the 2nd, 4th, 6th and such other alternate rows are planted midway between the 1st, 3rd 5th and such other alternate rows.

Trichome: An outgrowth of the epidermis which plays an important role in the water economy of the plant as seen in lower epidermis of succulent leaf.

Trickle irrigation: Syn. Drip irrigation

Trifoliate: A leaf divided in to three leaflets.

Trophy: An arrangement of colorful potted plants, annual or herbaceous perennials in different tiers around a central object which may be a tree trunk, lamp post or a pillar.

Tropophyte: A plant that is adapted to a climate characterized by a very dry season followed by a wet one.

True lithophytes: Plants that are capable of growing on bare, inclined rock surfaces, *e.g.*, lichen, moss *etc.*

True-over dominance: It is simply the phenomenon of over dominance which refers to the heterosis at a single locus.

Trug: A shallow basket for light chores, like carrying flowers and fruits and veggies. Traditionally made out of wood.

Trumpet: When the tepals are fused or appearing to be fused into the flared bell of a trumpet as in *Hymenocallis, Narcissus, etc.*

Trunk: The main stem of a tree usually bearing the primary branches.

Truss: A flower head or tightly packed inflorescence.

Tuber: Tuber is a specialized kind of swollen underground modified stem structure with a terminal and several lateral eyes, which functions as storage organ. The important examples are *Anemone, Begonia, Caladium, Dioscorea, Gloriosa* and *Musa.*

Tuberous root: Tuberous root include several type of stem structure with thickened tuberous growth that function as storage organ. The buds are formed at the crown or proximal end and the roots at the distant end. The important examples are *Dahlia, Eranthis, Ipomoea, Mirabilis, Ranunculus* and *Tapioca.*

Tuberous stem: Tuberous stem is the stem structure produced by the enlargement of the hypocotyls of seeding plant and the eyes are formed on all through the swollen organ. The important examples are *Begonia* and *Cyclamen.*

Tuberous: Producing tuber or resembling a tuber.

Tuff: Volcanic ash usually more or less stratified and in various states of consolidation.

Tunic: The papery or fibrous coats covering bulbs and corms.

Tunicate: Enclosure of a tunic, the papery covering of a bulb or a corm.

Tunicated bulbs: Type of bulb where the outer leaves are usually thin, membranous and dry and completely ensheath the inner portion and the central axis of the bulb like a tunic.

Turf crops: Low, usually perennial, plants such as grasses and creeping legumes, grown for lawns, parks, parkways, roadsides, *etc.* where an essentially complete cover of the ground is desired. *e.g.*, dubgrass, Bermuda grass, blue grass, dichondria, *etc.*

Turf plastering: A method of planting grass to develop a lawn in which a paste is prepared by mixing garden soil, fresh cowdung, bits of chopped-up fresh roots and stems or rhizomes of dub grass and water, and the paste is spread evenly on the surface of the prepared ground after moistening the soil.

Turf: A piece of land with grass thickly grown over it.

Turfing. A method of planning grass to develop a lawn in which a plate is prepared by mixing garden soil, fresh cowdung, bits of chopped-up fresh roots and stems or rhizomes of dub grass and water, and the paste is spread evenly on the surface of the prepared ground after moistening the soil.

Turgidity: Resistance to deformation of a water-containing tissue

Turgor movement: Movement of plant organs caused by reversible change in cell volume due to change in turgor.

Turgor [ressure: The pressure on a cell wall that is created from within the cell by the movement of water into it.

Turgor: The swollen condition of the cell resulting from the hydrostatic pressure exerted by the protoplast of the cell wall.

Turkscap: A type of lily flower in which the perianth segments roll back in a turban like manner.

Twin scaling: A propagation method in certain bulbs *e.g.* Narcissus where the bulbs are cut into many defined pieces and then separation of these pieces, with two small scale pieces attached to a part of the basal plate and planted in sterilized propagation medium such as vermiculite.

Twiner: Some climbing plant which do not have any special structures but climb over a support or a plant by twining themselves spirally around such supports is called twiner. *e.g.*, honeysuckle, madhavi, *etc.*

U

Umbel: Umbrella type inflorescence normally flat topped and corymb like where all the flowered pedicles arise from the same point at the apex of the axis.

Unilateral: Arranged only at one side.

Unity or harmony: It is an overall effect of various features, styles and colors of total scene. The unity in design is achieved by several ways: In simplest form, unity is expressed by the repetition of identical elements. Plants in the landscape should be limited in kind and variety in order to produce a unified effect as too many divergent shapes, textures or colours generate confusion, thus we can say that unity is achieved through various ways: First, the unity of style, feeling and function between the house and the garden. Second, the different components of the gardens should merge harmoniously with each other. Third, to achieve some harmony between the landscape and the garden, so that trains creepers on the porch to bring home close to the nature.

Upright style bonsai: Syn. Chokkan style bonsai.

Urban Design: Urban design is the process or act of arranging the both the appearance and functionality of a town or city to create safe and user friendly, public spaces. A subset of urban planning, urban design is a practice that involves a number of disciplines including issues such as urban economics, social theories, and also political economy

Urban Planning: Urban planning, as well as city and town planning are the integration of several disciplines regarding transport planning as well as land use planning. Urban planning explores a wide range of circumstances and aspects involving the environment and the surrounding communities. Urban planning might also have the primary goal of restoring or rebuilding inner city neighborhoods that have suffered from decay or lack of maintenance.

Urban Renewal: Urban renewal, sometimes referred to as urban regeneration, are programs that involve the redevelopment of land in areas of moderate to heavy urban usage. Having a large and positive impact on urban communities, urban renewal has played an important role throughout history in many cities all around the world. Despite the progress and its many supporters, some have disagreed with the practice of urban renewal citing issues such as urban sprawl, overpopulation, and the creation of too many freeways and expressways.

V

Vacuum cooling: A technique of cooling vegetables (leafy vegetables, asparagus, Brussels sprout, *etc.*) having a high surface to volume ratio rapidly and uniformly by boiling off some of their water at 1°C and at low pressure (5mm mercury) into a sealed container. The produce is cooled by evaporation of water from the tissue surface and is more rapid than hydro cooling.

Vacuum drier: A drier used to dry heat sensitive products where low pressure lowers the temperature which helps to retain natural flavour and minimizes oxidation and browning.

Vacuuming: The use of a vacuum/blower to clean the surface of the turf.

Value addition: Value addition is a process in which for the same volume of a primary product, a high price is realized by means of processing, packing, upgrading the quality or other such methods.

Value: Describes the colour intensity of hue.

VAM: It refers to vasicular-arbuscular mycorrhiza which play important role in growth of many crops like cocoa, pea, cowpea, citrus, *etc.*

Vanillin: The flavouring substance obtained from the cured, fully grown, unripe fruits of vanilla (*Vanilla planifolia*) which is used in flavouring chocolate, ice-cream, cakes, puddings *etc.*

Variants: Plants that are distinct within a variety but occur naturally in it and are originally a part of the variety as released, so the variants are not considered offtypes.

Variation: Differences among individuals belonging to a single species to different species. Variation may be due to genotype, environment, or both genotype and environment.

Variegated foliage: Leaves having various patterns of different colours other then green.

Variegated: Any variation in colour from the normal green Typically the condition where chloroplasts are absent from leaf tissue, resulting in a white or yellow appearance in the deficient region. The colour contrast of variegated plants makes them much prized.

Variegation: A characteristic of the leaves of many horticultural varieties in which there is more or less of a characteristic pattern due to alternating or scattered patches, areas, or stripes of different colours.

Varietal revamping: Re-establishment of a released variety which has run out of cultivation or deteriorated due to various reasons by secondary selection or other means.

Variety: A homogeneous group of plants related by descent but distinguished from other similar groups by characters too inconsistent or too trivial to recognize it as a species or whose distinguishing characters are controlled by the breeding approach.

Vascular cambium: A sheet like fundamental type of meristem that produces secondary xylem and phloem.

Vascular plants: Any species that has vascular tissue – xylem and phloem.

Vase life: The length of time that a cut flower retains its aesthetic value after it has been placed on display.

Vase solution: Syn. Holding solution.

Velamen: Spongy tissue covering the hanging aerial roots of epiphytic orchids which help the root to absorb atmospheric moisture.

Venation: Arrangement of the veins and the vein lets in the leaf blade.

Verge: A narrow strip of turf between beds, borders, paths walls *etc.*

Vermiculite: Common growing media component made from the mineral mica that has a good cation exchange capacity and neutral to slightly alkaline pH (6.3 -7.8).

Vernalization: A cold temperature treatment required by certain species in order to induce flowering.

Vernation: The arrangement of a leaf or leaves in the sheath. Vernation is often referred to as either rolled or folded.

Vertical garden: Vertical gardening involves gardening with upright structures so as to utilize the vertical space. It is ideal for gardening in the urban city areas and apartments with balconies. Many structures including fences, arbours, trellises and walls can be used to create vertical gardens. Hanging plants and pulley systems can be used to make vertical gardening attractive.

Vertical mowing or verti cutting: To remove some of the organic thatch buildup from the surface of the turf without interrupting the soil beneath turf is called vertical mowing. The process involves the tightly spaced rotating blades that cut vertically into the turf.

Vertical mulching: Incorporation of vegetative mulch in a band for the purpose of harvesting rain water and conserving soil and water.

Vertical resistance: Complete resistance to some races of a pathogen but not to others.

Vertical trimming: Vertical trimming or edging is necessary at regular intervals to maintain a neat appearance. Clippings should be removed from beds or borders after edging to prevent the bits of grass from rooting in the soil.

Viability: The ability of pollen, seed, *etc.* to live, grow and develop.

Viable seed: Seeds capable of producing normal healthy seedling under favourable conditions.

Victorian Era: The period during the reign of Queen Victoria of England known for establishing floral design as an art form and the language of flowers.

Virulence: The degree of pathogenicity of a pathogen.

Virus Indexing: A procedure used to determine whether a given plant is infected by a virus.

Visual balance: The perception of an arrangement looking aside.

Visual wcight: Perceived lightness or heaviness of plant material based upon its combined characteristics of colour, shape pattern, size, texture and spatial arrangement.

Vitrification in carnatlon: Problem will encounter during the In-vitro culture of carnation due to the formation of abnormal leaves and stem with thickened and translucent structures. Shoots with such abnormal leaves usually turn brown and failed to root in the rooting medium. Vitrification in carnation tissues, by transfer from solid to liquid medium was accompanied by decreased lignin content.

Vivipary: The phenomenon in which seed germinate in the fruit while it is still attached to the mother plant.

W

Warm hues: Red, Orange, Yellow and the tints shades and tones of other hues.

Warm-season plant: A plant that grows best at day time temperatures of between 18°-27° C.

Wash boarding: Wash boarding is a series of broad and regular corrugations running cross wise along the mown strip. It is caused by always mowing in the same direction.

Water garden: A shallow pond or lake of natural formation in which the water does not overflow its bounds in the rainy season or if it does, can be conveniently led away, leaving its level almost constant in the pond and beautified with aquatic ornamental plants or fish.

Water sprouts: A vigorous and vertical growing shoot produced on the trunk or branches of a tree.

Water stress: Occurs when a plant is unable to absorb adequate water to replace that lost by transpiration.

Water table: The upper surface of ground water that level below which the soil is saturated with water.

Weathering: Chemical and physical alteration of rocks and minerals resulting in their disintegration, decomposition and modification.

Wet storage of cut flowers: Short term storage of cut flowers where bases of flowers are held in water or in a preservative solution. It is ineffective in inhibiting the biological activity of flowers due to extensive water uptake, more carbohydrate depletion by respiration, *etc.*

Whip: A young tree seedling (about one year old) with a slender single stem (less than ½ inch wide)

Whorl: Three or more leaves, flowers or branches arranged in a circle at one point around the main stem.

Wild garden: This is comparatively a recent style of gardening. The revolutionary concept of 'wild garden' was expounded by William Robinson in the last decade of the nineteenth century. The concept of wild garden is not only against all formalism but it also breaks the rule of landscape styles. His main idea was to naturalize plants in shrubberies. He also preached that grass should remain unmowed, as in nature, and few bulbous plants should be grown scattered in the grass to imitate wild scenery.

Window gardening: 'Window gardening' or 'window-box gardening' is making of garden in the window sill or any other attachment to it.

Winter season annuals: These annuals are able to tolerate low temperature and there are about 100 winter season annuals. These are sown in September-November or February-April in hills.

Wintering: A management practice in rose in which pruning of shoots and exposing roots in the month of October to November is done and then the exposed roots area allowed to dry for about 7-10 days, afterwards the plants are manured and watered copiously. This treatment is practiced to induce healthy shoots which bear exhibition quality of flowers.

Wood: Secondary xylem.

Wreath: Flowers and foliages woven or fashioned into a circular shape.

Wrenching: Cutting of roots of a plant prior to lifting from the growing area.

Wrist corsage: A light weight corsage designed to be attached to a wristband for bearing on the wrist.

X

Xanthophylls: Yellow, hydroxyl carotene derivatives ($C_{40}H_{55}0_2$) which is present in all green leaves together with chlorophyll and carotene.

Xenia: Effect of the genotype of pollen grain on the phenotype of endosperm of the seed due to the phenomenon of double fertilization.

Xenogamy: Cross-Pollination between flowers borne in different plants.

Xeric: Dry applied to feature of plants or places where they grow.

Xeriscaping: It is the conservation of water through creative landscaping or a landscape installation strategy that groups plants according to water needs in order to improve irrigation efficiency.

Xerophytes: Plants which are adopted to live in drought conditions.

Xylem: Specialized cells through which water and minerals move upward inside the plant from the soil.

Xyloposis: Disorder associated with lack of compatibility between stock and scion.

Y

Yearling: One year old bulblets which has been formed on the scale.

Yose-ue-bonsai: When two or more bonsai plants are grown in a pot they are called yose-ue *i.e.*, trunks planted together. According to their number we may have Nihon-Yose two trunks planted together, Gohon-Yose five trunks planted together, and so on. The trees may be all of one kind or several kinds.

Z

Zebra stripes: Those alternate light and dark bands seen so often on mown lawns are taken by many people to be a sign of quality. These bands are the result of the lawn being cut in parallel stripes with a mower fitted with a roller, the alternate stripes being mown in opposite directions. An attractive technique especially as it helps to mask minor imperfections or colour variations, but it is unsightly if not done accurately and neatly.

Zelkova: One of the trees especially cultivated for its bare winter beauty is the gray-barked elm, or keyaki, *Zelkova serrata*. It makes a broad, round-topped head with dense branches, small elm-like leaves and handsome trunk to be suitable for bonsai.

Zeneibana: In this style a beautiful sculpture is created using wood, stone, rocks, metal depicting any natural scenery.

Zeneika: 'Zeneika' means abstract and this style does not stimulate nature. Straight material with uneven height is used.

Zygomorphic: An irregular flowering capable of being divided in half but in only one plane.

References

1. Arora, J.S. 2006. Introductory Ornamental Horticulture. Kalyani Publishers, Ludhiana, India.

2. Bose, T.K. and Mukherjee, D. 2004. Gardening in India. Oxford and IBH Publishers Co., Kolkata, India.

3. Bose, T.K. and Yadav, L.P. 1989. Commercial Flowers, Naya Prokash Publishers, Kolkata, India.

4. Bose, T.K., Maity, R.G., Dhua, R.S. and Das, P. 1999. Floriculture and Landscaping. Naya Prokash Publishers, Kolkata, India.

5. Brady, N.C., 1995. The Nature and properties of Soils. Macmillan Publishing Co, New York, USA.

6. Chaddha, K.L. 2001. Handbook of Horticulture. Directorate of Information and Publications of Agriculture, Pusa, New Delhi, India.

7. Gardner, E. J., Simmons, M.J. and Snustard, D.P. Principles of Genetics (VIII Edn). John Wiley and Sons, New York, USA.

8. Greenhouse Management. Training Manual. Horticulture Training Centre. National Institute of Post Harvest Technology's (NIPHT), Pune, India.

9. Grewal, H.S. and Parminder Singh. 2014. Landscape Designing and Ornamental Plants. Kalyani Publishers, Ludhiana, India.

10. Gupta, P.K. 1985. Cytology, genetics and cytogenetics. Rastogi Publications, India.

11. Hartmann, Hudson T., Dale E. Kester, Fred T. Davies, Jr. and Robert L. Geneve. Plant Propagation: Principles and Practices (7th Edition). Prentice Hall, Inc., New Jersy, USA.

12. Hazra, P., S.K. Ghosh, T. K. Maity and M. G. Som.2001. Glossary of Horticulture. Kalyani Publishers, New Delhi.

13. Hessayon, D.G. 2006. The Bulb Expert. Transworld Publishers. 61-63 Uxbridge Road, London, U.K.

14. Hessayon, D.G. 2007. The Lawn Expert. Transworld Publishers. 61-63 Uxbridge Road, London, U.K.

15. Raj Desh. 2004 Floriculture at a Glance. Kalyani Publishers, Ludhiana, India.

16. Randhawa, G.S. and Mukhopadhyay, A. 2004. Floriculture in India. Allied Publishers, New Delhi, India.

17. Salaria, A.S and Salaria B.S. 2010. Intellects's A2Z-Horticulture at a glance-III. Floriculture Landscape Gardening and Medicinal and Aromatic Plants. INTELLECTS-Nature to Excel, New Delhi, India.

18. Salisbulry. 2007. Plant Physiology. CBS, New Delhi, India.

19. Singh, B.D. 1983. Plant Breeding Principles and Methods. Kalyani Publishers, New Delhi, India.

20. Singh, J. 2002. Basic Horticulture. Kalyani Publishers, New Delhi, India.

21. Swarup, V. 1990. Garden Flowers. National Book Trust, New Delhi, India.

22. Tiwari, A.K. and R. Kumar. 2012. Fundamentals of Ornamental Horticulture and Landscape Gardening. New India Publishing Agency, New Delhi, India.

23. Trivedi, D. 1975. Ikebana. Vikas Publishing House, New Delhi, India.